Ham Bones: memoirs of a southern cook
© 2015 J. D. McDuffie, all rights reserved

Published by MarFran Fitz Press
Paperback ISBN: 978-0-578-16836-4
Hardcover ISBN: 978-0-578-16835-7
Library of Congress Control Number: 2015911908

First Edition August 2015

Cover design, book design & layout, and ebook conversion by
www.jimandzetta.com

Requests for permissions or other information may be sent to the author at jmcduff50@gmail.com

Table of Contents

~ o0o ~

in loving memory of
the two best southern cooks
I have known!

my wonderful mother
Dorothea Ernestine ("Bunch") Brownlee McDuffie
(1922 – 1996)

and

her wonderful sister
who taught her the proper
way of cooking good food

Emma Tecora ("Emma T") Brownlee Harrison
(1919 - 1985)

Acknowledgements

~ o0o ~

It is very clear to me that it has taken well over sixty years to write this book! But, even so, this writing could not have taken place if my many family members and loving friends had not consented to be my test palates! There are so many people to express sincere gratitude for all the accolades received when a dish was great; and the same expression of gratitude for the gracious tact when much improvement was warranted!

As I think back over the years of my cooking, many friends consented to be dinner guests without early notice beforehand! Family members have allowed themselves to be guinea pigs just to see if something I was thinking would end up as a good result.

Before all the testing and the inviting over at the last minute, there were the lessons to be had; and on that score I think I had two of the best teachers – a wonderful mother who seem to have no boundaries when it came to cooking adventures; and one of her exceptionally competent sisters, a home economist that taught many a farmers' wives how to cook and preserve their bounty. It is from the foundation that these two cookin' divas gave me that I can take some ham bones and feed ya'!

Through the years, I have had the pleasure of knowing some wonderful folks that have encouraged me to write this book. Some have cooked my recipes several times and reported back on the consistency of results. Paramount among those is a life-long friend, the accomplished actress Margo Moorer. Our second-generation friendship has spanned the decades; and though a busy professional as a character actress in such films as "Forrest Gump"; and the "The Watsons Go to Birmingham"; or trekking back and forth to New York City to see her daughter Amber Iman perform in "Soul Doctor", she would also find the time to cook my recipes! I took the liberty of lovingly tagging her "my favorite test chef" as she tested so many of these recipes! As she and her husband love the turkey wings so much, I've named them "Turkey Wings Margo"! As you examine the recipe, note that although I've done them with turkey wings, you'll conclude that most fowl wings will result in similar delicious results.

Holiday potluck office parties during my days as an accounting professor turned out to be a great venue to try out a cake here or a pie there—especially on my students who made their way to my residence to raid my refrigerator! Sunday dinners after church with the family of my God sons were terrific because their mother Kathy and I just loved to talk about food! Their Dad Jeryl loved my bar-b-que sauce, so he loved summer dinners! I was introduced to soft-shell crabs in New York City by friends Dave and Lynne. Even now, when on the east coast, I anticipate with much excitement the short season for which the crabs are available with those soft shells. These are wonderful friends of many wonderful years' duration with whom I have enjoyed cooking and dining and who have kept me on the busy to get this book finished!

Two little girls that loved to spend a weekend with their Uncle Bubba so that they could make brownies and cookies for their other two uncles grew up to be wonderful ladies that know their way around the kitchen as well. Marilynn and Cessa continue to show their appreciation for good southern food, and are forever inquisitive about what will happen if a little bit of this or a little bit of that is added to or taken from of an old recipe. A catalyst for writing this book had a lot to do with frequent inquiries for Grandma Bunch's recipes! Many times, they have come up with wonderful dishes that are all their own.

Though there are many other family members and friends to whom it would be appropriate to express gratitude, I realize that no matter how many I name, there would always continue to be just as many that I would have forgotten to mention. Accepting the shortcoming of my memory, I take the liberty of expressing gratitude to all who have eaten so many of my dishes; lauded approval; and have come back for seconds for all these many years!

With great respect for the cooking during my formative years, I have written this book with vivid memories of my elders advising me to always appreciate this food. As I sit and reminisce, I can still see my Uncle Isaiah at a family gathering for a holiday dinner! Having completed a wonderful meal, he always found it proper to rare back a tad bit to show the increase of the bulge of his stomach and thus compliment the cooks with "that was some righteous good eatin'"!

Though they knew an inquiry was unnecessary, the cooks of the bodacious holiday meal would always inquire: "...did y'all get enough to eat?" With anticipation of the inquiry, always as in unison, the men-folk at the table would reply: "It was A Gracious Plenty, thank you!"

J. D. McDuffie
Duncanville, TX
July 2015

Introduction

Southern is much more than living here; it's also a state of mind; it's pride in one's roots and family tree; it's hospitality and kindness towards others without much limitation!

Below the Mason-Dixon line, it's geographic for sure – but, the love of a good ham bone for seasoning one's pot of upcoming goodness; a gracious plenty of macaroni & cheese casserole and a good heap of well-seasoned, tender collard greens; along with the smacking of lips and licking of fingers after eating fried chicken will make you southern enough!!!

Whether gathering recipes for this book, or writing a recipe for a new dish I had created, one thing always seem to be a part of the process: Fond family memories of times past! So many stories came to mind. I've shared some of these stories as well as some anecdotes as a means of introducing you to so that you can *meet"* some of the cooks and members of my family as you cook and enjoy their dishes!

Growing up, I was so lucky that there were so many good cooks in our family. Yet, the cooking from my Mother's side of the family differed a bit from my Daddy's side of the family. So, I've separated them a bit in writing this book. I've introduced them to you through little chats and stories as if we might be sitting on the front porch enjoying an early morning cup of coffee; or an evening bourbon while enjoying the stars of an early spring or fall evening. But, you have to promise not to tell the saintly women-folks in the family that we are out on the front porch partaking of spirits!!!

Part One – Emma T and Bunch!

These are some dishes from my mother's side of the family. My mother got immense pleasure spending a Saturday with her older sister, Emma T as the two of them resigned themselves to the kitchen cooking and talking – just having a grand ol' time as close sisters enjoy each other's company. This is the initial introduction of my family's southern cooking and some of the first foods I enjoyed as cooked by *"Emma T and Bunch!"*

Part Two – The Sisters Finch!

My daddy's people could cook pretty darn well too! So, in the second section I've written about some of their cooking and present some of their dishes as well. They were from a line of family farmers in the Gadsden/Kingsville area of Richland County, South

Carolina. They were of the Finch Clan! My Grand-mother Corrie and her sisters Lucille, Clotelle, and Ivy Lee were the ones that I remember. Of special note is my Grandmother's stove-top huckleberry dumpling that I would eat 'til I hurt if I could get away with it; and Aunt Lucille's Garden Fresh Tomato Onion Soup! Also, one of their cousins Estelle was just somebody really special when it came to commandeering a kitchen! Her coconut cake was a divine poem; blessings upon the palate!

Part Three – Fly Away Home!

Everybody has to grow up; and sometimes leave home to far away places. I was no different than most, and found myself enjoying many other cuisines as a result of my travels and setting up different homes in different places. Like all birds that leave the nest, I grew into my own, spreading my wings of a sort when it came to cooking. In this section I've included some of the dishes that I created and taken back home for my family to enjoy. Many of these dishes have become an addition to the family-recipes file.

So, what do ya' say we put together some basic kitchen tools; get some pantry essentials; and go into the kitchen and do some southern cookin'?!

Some Kitchen Essentials

~ o0o ~

When setting up a kitchen, one of the things that should always be kept in mind is cost. No matter your personal finances, budgeting is an essential financial discipline when making decisions about acquiring essential tools and equipment.

Many items are single-purpose, and I have always tried to avoid them whenever possible. I think you get far more bang for your buck when you are able to do more than one thing with an individual item. With this concept in mind, I list some items that I think you should definitely have as part of your basic kitchen tools keeping in mind that as you expand your cooking adventures, so shall you desire and acquire more tools.

I have found that the pretty stuff is okay for the dining room where a visually-exciting tablescape may be the goal; but when standing over a hot stove, pretty is not as important as is utility! I also find that good quality tools provide reliable service for longer periods of time than flimsy inferior merchandise that you can get on the cheap. I like commercial-grade quality for many of my cooking essentials, and out of habit, have a tendency to frequent my local restaurant-supply store.

I suggest that you include these items as part of your kitchen set up:

Knives, Forks & Spoons

I don't think a woodblock of 10 or 12 knives serve any useful purpose in the kitchen. I have such a set and find it was a great waste of money! When I look at that set, I am reminded that many of life's lessons can be rather expensive!

You will have your essential knife needs if you have –

a)   medium-size chef knife
b)   medium-size serrated knife
c)   a paring knife
d)   a boning knife and
e)   a pair of excellent kitchen shears

You should be certain to pick up spoons that you can use for cooking, as well as take to the table later for serving. Spoons can be inexpensive, but should be sturdy and of notable weight.

2-3 spoons should be slotted
2-3 spoons should be solid
2-3 wooden spoons are a must
2-3 meat forks are essential
Tongs for meat should be of various sizes

Pots and Pans

Whether you buy non-stick versus no-coating is a personal preference. I have both and use them for different reasons when cooking different things. I like the non-stick when I'm cooking an omelet. I have little use for it if I'm frying up some bacon!

You should be sure that you have a –

Small-size fry pan
Medium-size fry pan
Large-size fry pan
3 sauce pots (small, medium and large)
2 half-sheet pans
2 quarter-sheet pans
2 half-size steam-table pans
1 quarter-size steam-table pans

The fry pans as well as the square and rectangular deep-dish hot table pans should all have available lids for them. You will do well to get the lids. Lids are especially nice when you want to keep something in the fridge overnight in the pan in which you intend to bake, or already baked! Cornbread dressing and meatloaf for the half-size and quarter-size steam-table pans come to mind!

You may find that your local feed and seed store, or hardware store, is the best source for reasonably-priced cast-iron. You'd want to have at least a 12-inch cast-iron fry pan; a 9-inch cast-iron fry pan; a round or square grill with the ridges for doing steaks and chops.

The one piece of cast-iron that will not be a price-bargain item will be an enameled cast-iron Dutch Oven. It will be necessary to splurge a bit, so only buy one. It should be a bit on the large size, which will be rather heavy, but wonderful to have for braising and stews!

Measuring cups and spoons

Commercial measuring cups are great to have about, especially when baking cakes. A pound cake that calls for four cups of flour could be measured in one pass! What is essential is that you have both dry-measure and liquid-measure cups, as well as measuring spoons. Again, the commercial quality you will find the commercial quality to be long-lasting. You will want a variety from 4-cups down to ⅓and ¼-cup sizes.

Sifters

I like a commercial, 8-cup large sifter with the crank handle on the side and the rotating prongs/

arms inside the unit. A smaller one of about the 4 to 6-cup size would be a good extra unit.

(An essential caveat: Never ever wet your sifter! I keep mind in a plastic bag that is kept in a brown paper bag! After I sift my flour, I tap it to release residual flour left in its basket. It is returned to its bags for storage in my cabinet until needed again. I have the same sifters I bought 25 or so years ago. They look as good as the day they were purchased. None of my sifters have been exposed to water!)

Other tools

A planer for zesting citrus fruit is essential
A mandolin is needed, and a high-end plastic one will suffice
A vegetable peeler, and food-mill (I like Oxo products)
Several whisks of various sizes from miniature to large
Small counter-top coffee grinder that serves double duty (i.e., relieves me of the need of a mortar and pestle.) Cuisinart also makes a small chopper/ grinder food processor that is quite reasonable in price. I am sure that there are others out there as well, I just happen to mention what I actually have in my kitchen!

Bowls

When setting up, be sure and purchase several stainless steel bowls. They are very economical, and 2 or 3 small, medium, large and one extra large size will serve you well.

For a large, old-fashion ceramic mixing bowl, you will find gourmet kitchen stores to be the best place to find them. My mother, her sisters, and all other great cooks that I know who bake bread, love these bowls. They are large and heavy and will remind you of times you watched your grandmother's bread-making in her kitchen!

Mixers and blenders

The cooks in my family all insisted on the Sunbeam Mixmaster mixer. And, of course, I have one as well. I do a bit more baking than my mother did; even more than my aunt, the home economist. So, I have acquired a bit of a mixer collection!

If you have one good-quality mixer, that should suffice you. I like both Kenwood and Viking 7-quarts, so I have both of them. I have friends who love the KitchenAid line of mixers and are likewise, very loyal to that brand. The thing about mixers – get what pleases you, as a good-quality mixer will last you for many years. But, take care to buy wisely – mixers are a high-dollar item. To be sure, spend the money but, don't get an inferior mixer!

I am of the same mindset when it comes to blenders. I have a commercial blender. Waring and Hamilton Beach make two of the best ones. They have one metal toggle handle, two speeds and will do anything you need done! None of that plastic housing with the dozen little push buttons! Think of the blenders you see in your local bar for mixing drinks—they are heavy duty and last a long time! That's what I wanted! I advise the same for your needs as well.

Some Pantry Essentials

~ o0o ~

I almost always make my own spice blends and rubs for seasoning; but I do think that too many varieties of spices can be over-kill and end up not giving you the taste results you want in a final dish. There will be occasion when you will need a special spice that you do not keep on hand; that's typical of any pantry. However, there are some basic spices and staples that you should have in your kitchen that will serve you well when preparing the recipes I am sharing with you. When I name a brand, it is only to inform you of what I use in particular. You may like a different brand of the same spice or sauce – that is fine; it should not change the results of the dish being prepared.

Table salt – (I use iodized salt)
Sea Salt
Rock salt – (I usually buy this during the summer when making ice cream)
Black pepper – (I buy ground [coarse & fine]; as well as whole peppercorns)
Red pepper flakes
Cayenne pepper

Dried spices & herbs (parsley flakes; oregano;
thyme; sage)
Onion powder
Granulated onion
Garlic powder
Granulated garlic
Dry mustard
Paprika (Hungarian; and Spanish)
Turmeric
Coriander
Cumin
Chili powder
Old Bay Seasoning (a great prepared mix that I
use)
Texas Pete Hot Sauce
Texas Pete Pepper Sauce
McIlhenny Tobasco Sauce (red)
Lea & Perrins Worcestershire Sauce
Soy Sauce
Prepared minced Horseradish (refrigerated jars)
Molasses
Pure maple syrup
Dark Brown Sugar
Light Brown Sugar
10-x Confectioners' Sugar
Granulated sugar (superfine)
Baking powder
Baking soda
Corn starch
Pure vanilla extracts *(I like both Madagascar and*

*Mexican varieties. I **<u>never</u> <u>ever</u>** use imitation vanilla flavor!)*
Pure lemon extract
Pure orange extract
Maple flavoring
Rum flavoring
Coconut flavoring
Red Food coloring
Yellow Food coloring
Dried peas and beans (lentils; field peas; limas; black-eyed peas; kidney; pinto; navy; black; green-pea; 12- or 15-bean mix for soups)
Long-grain converted rice
Bread crumbs (Italian and plain)
Panko bread crumbs

~ I ~
Emma T & Bunch

~ o0o ~

There were 14 siblings and more than 20 years between the oldest and the youngest. My mother "Bunch" was the youngest. The sister next to her was "Emma T", whom we called Aunt Emma T

Their mother died when my mother was but a few months over two years old. The oldest sister, whom we called Aunt Sister, took mother and raised her the way she knew their mother would have done. Growing up, Bunch was very close to Aunt Emma T, and all through life they were like two peas in a pod – the best of friends.

Aunt Emma T was very pious and soft-spoken. She was the most kind-hearted angel of the family that would give you her last if she thought it would help you! She was a home economist in the early part of her career in education, and would travel in the rural areas to teach farmers' wives essential food preparation and storage. Her husband, Uncle Isaiah, had an agriculture degree and would teach the farmers about their crops; animal husbandry; proper hog slaughtering techniques and the like! They were quite the couple and well known by most of the farmers in the rural communities of Orangeburg County. Uncle Isaiah being a big-time deacon in the country church in which he grew up, they were also well-known in the Baptist churches in those communities!

All of the siblings deferred to "Emma T" as the authority on all matters about food and cooking; and when in doubt, consulted her. She held court on food matters intermittently on weekends in her kitchen when convenient for the sibling sisters to come over for coffee and a chat! I fondly remember those sisters having such a ball at those "court sessions" as though they had been anticipating the gathering for weeks!

My two brothers and I, when not running through the house imitating westerns favorites with our cap pistols, would be in the back yard climbing the chinaberry tree! Wouldn't be long before one of the grown ups come out to summons us in for Aunt Emma T's "sample" with a cold glass of milk! This was always quite the treat, because any time those sisters got together, making one of Aunt Emma T's All-Butter Pound Cakes was a given. Though the cake had been made many times and they knew the recipe like the back of their hands; it was a given that a sample be made to determine if adjustments were required for the final batter! We'd love when mother would be planning a visit to Aunt Emma T because we knew that there would be a batter bowl to lick; and a warm sample to eat with an ice cold glass of milk!

I still have memories of my aunt making this cake! The sisters would be sitting around her kitchen table chatting while the butter and sugar was creaming in the Mixmaster! Never missing an opportunity to teach a lesson, the chat was always a repeat lecture, with demonstration, on how to measure flour for the cake. Her famous words before demonstrating: "Measure as I am about to measure for this pound cake we are making!" Of course, "we" were not making anything – she never let anyone assist with the making of her dishes – you may watch – but "do not disturb the pots"!

Her technique for measuring the flour—*sifting into the cup*! This was an unbending, hard and fast rule she had about baking cakes. I still laugh when I think of a comment my mother made to her one time regarding this rule: "Emma T why can't I just stir the flour and lightly spoon it in to the measuring cup and level off?" My aunt's reply: "That will be fine if all you want is some sweetnin' bread!"

That being said, she then reminded my mother of the technique: Lay out two sheets of wax paper on the counter; have your sifter resting on one sheet; your small ingredient bowl on the other sheet, along with your box of cake flour, and your icing spatula for leveling off the flour once measured. Next, spoon your flour into the sifter; filling up the sifter is suggested. With the sifter held over the measuring cup, *sift the flour into the measuring cup* until you have a "mountain peak" of flour. Sit the sifter down; use the spatula to level off the measured flour; and pour it into the ingredient bowl. Repeat this process until the correct amount of flour has been measured. For returning the excess flour to the cake-flour box, use the wax paper as a funnel!

Aunt Emma T was very clear that this kind of precision was not required when making biscuits and cornbreads as they are a dough or batter whereby sight and feel is a part of the recipe!

On alternating Sundays, Aunt Emma T would be going to Uncle Isaiah's family church in the country. Ever so frequently, certain Sundays would be set aside as the great meeting of the association of "sister" churches. Those meetings were called the "union"! Whenever my brothers and I would hear about the "union", we would insist that we go to church with Uncle Isaiah and Aunt Emma T on that particular upcoming Sunday! We knew the deal: Church ladies from all those churches with all that food! All those cakes, cookies, potato salad, Cole slaw, fried chicken were forever on our minds!

Of course, the "union" was for serious church association business. But, you'd never know it by the way we (i.e., my two brothers and I) acted! You'd think that our family never fed us at home! My two brothers, Brownie and Wallace took it upon themselves as a sacred Christian duty to make sure that there was good quality of all food brought to the "union"; and they preferred the sampling method! And to be sure, they found that random statistical sampling was not sufficient; but instead, each and every dish should be critiqued! No matter how many times we were told prior to leaving the house, to eat at our table as Aunt Emma T always prepared more than enough food – my two brothers were insistent upon that not being Christian-like! Breaking bread together should be repeated as often as possible, and at as many tables as possible! *(So much for all that wonderful home training we got at home!)*

There could never be a church union unless there were at least three or four Deacons to inquire on behalf of their wives and family as to whether Miss Emma T would be bringing along one of her All-Butter Pound Cakes to the meeting?! Of course, Aunt Emma T would always take the inquiry as a hint that more than one of her cakes would be needed!

4

~ I ~ Emma T & Bunch

Her pound cake was the very first cake she taught my mother to bake! It is the first cake that she and my mother taught me to bake! It is the very first recipe that I should have in my memoirs of those days!

If everyone met up at one house for a big family holiday dinner, a typical menu probably consisted of a roasted turkey; mother's cinnamon baked ham; and any assortment of a variety of vegetables. Aunt Sister, though not being the great cook in the family, was known for her green beans that she called "Kentucky Wonders". Any time we had a family-gathering dinner, the first request to the family "matriarch": "Sister, be sure and make plenty of your "Kentucky Wonders!"

Of course, Sunday dinners at home always included fried chicken – a southern ritual! Mother made her fried chicken just a little bit different from Aunt Emma T; and I make mine just a little bit different from theirs! My version is in the "Fly Away Home" section.

Aunt Emma T's
All-Butter Pound Cake

(Note: A flavorful velvet-textured pound cake that was a family favorite.)

In making this pound cake, you'll want to have a large, heavy pound-cake pan with the removable tube-bottom! Some folks call this an angel-cake pan! Butter and flour it, then let it rest in the refrigerator while you are making the batter.

If your children are looking up at you as you finish filling the cake pan with batter, they are advising you of their property rights! The bowl belongs to them for fingering and licking their fingers! Show some love – please accommodate 'em!

Bake at: 350° - 1 hour, 15 minutes
– test for doneness!

4 sticks (one pound) unsalted butter
2 teaspoons pure vanilla extract
1 ¼ cups whole milk
9 large eggs
2 cups granulated sugar
4 cups cake flour
2 teaspoons baking powder
½ teaspoon iodized table salt

Instructions:

1. Butter and flour a tube pound-cake pan and sit in refrigerator to rest.
2. Cream the butter, then add the sugar.
3. Cream again – now with the sugar – until light and fluffy.
4. Add the vanilla and cream some more until blended/incorporated.
5. Add one egg at the time, cream until blended/incorporated. Repeat process until all eggs are added.
6. In a bowl that you have sifted the flour, use a whisk and slowly stir in the baking powder and salt – make sure it is well blended.
7. Add large serving-spoon-size amounts of the blended flour to the creamed butter sugar egg mixture, alternating with the milk.
8. When complete, the batter should have the appearance of a very elegant custard. (Do not over mix the batter!)
9. Pour into pound-cake tube pan. Tap the pan once or twice to remove air pockets in the batter!
10. Bake until done! Let cool in the tube pan for at least 2 hours before removing to a cake plate.

This cake also accepts an icing very well. My mother would add a vanilla butter cream to her finished pound cake. (In a bowl she would whip together 1 stick of butter; 1 teaspoon of vanilla extract; 1 pound of 10-X confectioner's sugar; and half & half milk sparingly to get the desired consistency she wanted for spreading the icing on the cake.)

Bunch's
Cinnamon-Baked Ham
(with pineapple-orange glaze)

Mother use to season this ham and leave it in the refrigerator overnight for all the seasonings to permeate the meat. The end result – absolutely delicious!

Pre-heat oven at: 500°
Bake covered at 350° for 1 hour, 30 minutes
or more dependent upon the size of the ham.

Glaze then continue to bake uncovered at 250° for 30 minutes.

This recipe calls for **a whole hardwood smoked ham** with skin on it.

For the Spice Mix:
4 TABLEspoons each of –
salt, pepper
paprika
dried orange peel
dry mustard powder
cinnamon
ground cloves

~ I ~ Emma T & Bunch

<u>For the Glaze:</u>
1 cup light brown sugar
½ cup granulated sugar
¼ cup apple cider vinegar
1 cup pineapple juice
1 cup frozen orange juice concentrate
¼ cup cornstarch
½ stick unsalted butter
1 cup pineapple tidbits
1 teaspoon crushed red pepper flakes

plus ¼ of the spice mix, which would be –
1 TABLEspoons each of – salt, pepper, paprika, dried
orange peel, dry mustard powder, cinnamon
ground cloves

<u>Season the ham:</u>
1. In a bowl combine the Spice Mix..
2. Carefully remove skin from the ham, then score fat in a diamond pattern.
3. Sprinkle ¾ of the seasoning mix liberally on all sides of the ham. Then, refrigerate the ham for at least 4 hours; preferably overnight.
4. Save the remaining ¼ of the seasoning mix to make the glaze.

<u>Make the glaze:</u>
In a sauce pot combine all glaze ingredients and simmer until thickened. Then set aside to cool to be used after the ham bakes!

To bake the ham:

1. Sit the seasoned ham on a rack in a roasting pan. Add 1 cup of apple pineapple juice and 1 cup of water in the pan. Cover and bake the ham covered for one hour and thirty minutes; more dependent upon size of ham.
2. Remove the ham from the oven, uncover and let it rest for 20 minutes.
3. Brush the glaze on the ham liberally! Then return the ham to the oven and let it continue to bake uncovered at 250° for 30 minutes.
4. Remove the glazed ham from the oven and let it rest at least 30 minutes before slicing.

Aunt Sister's
Kentucky Wonders

These green beans are so good when cooked very slowly, over a low heat! When Aunt Sister made these for family-gathering dinners, there was never a problem with getting children to eat their vegetables! Aunt Sister's recipe makes a plenty, which was a good thing because folks always wanted a second helping!

About 3 pounds of fresh big flat green beans *(Aunt Sister called these "Kentucky Wonders"; but, I now know these as Italian green beans!)*
4 large Russet white potatoes – peeled and cut into medium-size cubes
3 slices thick hickory-smoked bacon cut into thirds
1 slice salt pork (streak-o-lean)

Seasoning Mix: 1 TABLEspoon each
pepper, granulated sugar + 1 teaspoon red pepper flakes

1 small onion – finely minced
1 clove garlic – finely minced
2 teaspoons white vinegar
4 cups water

Instructions:

1. Wash the beans; set aside and let drain on paper towels
2. In a Dutch Oven or large stock pot slowly cook the three slices of bacon (there should be 9 pieces, as you would have cut these into thirds!) along with the 1 slice of salt pork (streak-o-lean). Once cooked, remove and set aside on a paper towel.
3. Leave about 3 TABLEspoons of the pork fat in the pot and drain off the rest!
4. Add 1 cup of the water and bring to a hard boil. With a wooden spoon scrape up all the bacon goodies in the bottom of the pot.
5. Add the seasoning mix along with the minced onion and garlic and the vinegar, and the remaining 3 cups of water. Bring to a hard boil and add the green beans. When the pot comes to a hard boil again with the green beans, turn heat down, cover and simmer for ½ hour.
6. Add the cut potatoes and continue to simmer covered for 1 hour. Remove cover and turn heat up to medium and cook for another ½ hour UNcovered and reduce the liquid by half.
7. Remove from heat, scatter both the cooked bacons atop the beans/potatoes and let sit covered for 20 minutes before serving.

Aunt Emma T's
Brined Roasted Turkey

This recipe calls for a 12-16 pound turkey! Rather than use a turkey any bigger, our family prefers to cook more than one turkey. Super large turkeys don't seem to be as tender as those in the 12-16 pound weight range.

For the brine:
1 ½ cups, (flaked) Kosher salt
1 ¼ cups, brown sugar
10 whole cloves *or* 1 TABLEspoon ground cloves
3 teaspoons, black peppercorns *or* 2 teaspoons of coarse black pepper
1 gallon water; 2 quarts apple juice; 1 can frozen orange juice (thawed)
the peel from one orange (skin only - no white pith – use a planer and zest it)
3 teaspoons, dried thyme and/or 3 teaspoons, dried sage; 3 teaspoons of dry mustard powder

Instructions:

Combine all ingredients in a non-reactive pot, bring mixture to a boil, lower heat and simmer for 15-20 minutes (partly covered). Allow brine to cool completely.

I rush this by putting in some ice (usually the full bin from the icemaker!) Since I use my cooler to brine, I simply put the mixture and the ice in the cooler before submerging the turkey.

Rinse turkey under cool running water, inside and out (remove giblets from body cavity). Pat turkey dry with paper towels, then immerse turkey in cooled brine.* Turkey should be completely submerged in liquid (place a plate on top of the bird if necessary to keep it covered with the liquid).

Close the cover and let the turkey remain in the brine for 8-10 hours or up to 24 hours. (Continue to check the turkey every four hours to make sure that there the brine is cool to the touch. If needed, add more ice.) After 24 hours, remove turkey, rinse, pat dry, season and roast the turkey.

For a crispy skin:
After removing the turkey from the brine, rinsing it and patting it dry, allow the turkey to stand UNCOVERED in the refrigerator for 6-12 hours or overnight. This will dry the skin and result in its being crispy at serving time. Just before going in the oven, brush it with melted butter; sprinkle with salt, pepper, garlic powder, dry mustard, orange peel! Stuff cavity with quartered onion, celery and carrots and a couple of apples and roast uncovered! You won't believe the flavor at the end!

This resting period has the added advantage of evening the degree of brininess throughout the meat (it will be less salty on the surface of the meat, more evenly brined throughout), and resting produces a slightly more tender result.

For a SUPER-moist turkey:

Aunt Emma T's technique was to initially turn the oven up to 500 degrees and get it very hot. Roast the turkey at 500 degrees UN-covered for 15-20 minutes to get a nice brown skin. (Watch it, don't let it burn spots on the turkey!) Lift up the turkey in order to add 2 cups of water in the roasting pan, 1 cup each of chopped onion, celery and carrots in the bottom of the pan. Then sit turkey on rack back down in the roasting pan, cover and roast/bake at 210-220 for 5 to 6 hours.

Usually, I do this about 2:00 a.m. and go to bed! When I wake up in the morning, the turkey will be fully cooked and super-moist!!!!!!!!!

Family Fried Chicken

Mother and Aunt Emma T both had wonderful fried chicken. They both used similar spices as well as peanut oil for frying their chicken. Their variations are below.

This recipe calls for – 1 medium-size chicken, cut up for frying

Dry Ingredients:
3 cups plain flour
1 TABLEspoon each of – salt, pepper, poultry seasoning, paprika

Getting ready to fry:
Aunt Emma T would fry two or three slices of hickory-smoked bacon in her fry pan for the rendered bacon fat. Remove the bacon once cooked, then pour peanut oil into a large cast-iron fry pan and heat the oil to 360-degrees; then turn it down to 325 degrees for actual frying of the chicken.

Aunt Emma T's method:
1. Wash chicken and pat dry.
2. Sprinkle seasoning on chicken and let it rest for 30 minutes in refrigerator.

3. Then, coat chicken with the flour; let sit for a minute to adhere – then coat chicken again and fry in hot oil until done.

Mother's method:

Mother did not use bacon fat – only peanut oil.

1. Wash chicken and pat dry.
2. *Add seasoning to flour*; put in zip-lock bag and shake and mix.
3. After it is mixed well, then pour into an oblong pan and let it sit there.
4. *Combine 1 egg and 1 cup of whole milk in bowl.*
5. Dip chicken in milk/egg wash, then dredge in seasoned flour.
6. Let sit for a minute to adhere; dip in egg wash again; then dredge in flour again.
7. Fry slowly in hot oil until done.

Candied Yams

Whenever Mother's candied yams were part of Sunday dinner, we considered it an extra dessert! These are sweet and spicy with a hint of orange.

Preheat oven on 350° - Bake 1 hour 30 minutes on 350°

5 - 6 medium-size yams
¼ cup water
¼ cup orange juice
½ stick unsalted butter or margarine

in a small bowl combine:
½ cup light brown sugar
¼ cup granulated sugar
¼ cup granulated sugar separately
1 TABLEspoon each – cinnamon, nutmeg, fresh orange zest
1 teaspoon each – ground ginger, ground cloves

Instructions:

1. Wash and slice the yams length-wise medium-thick *(a mandolin would be quite handy for this task)*.
2. Use ¼ stick of butter to grease a 9 x 13 oven-safe baking dish.

3. Sprinkle ¼ cup granulated sugar to coat the butter.
4. Put a layer of sliced yams in the dish.
5. Liberally spoon half of the mixed spice & sugar seasoning on the yams.
6. Dot with the ½ of the remaining butter or margarine.
7. Put another layer of sliced yams in the dish.
8. Liberally spoon the remaining mixture of the spice & sugar seasoning.
9. Dot with the remaining butter or margarine.
10. Combine the orange juice and water; sprinkle ½ over the yams.
11. Pour the remainder in the corner of the dish so as not to wash off the spicy sugar.
12. Bake covered for 1 hour until yams are semi-done
13. Bake UNcovered for 30 minutes to set the "candy" on the yams

MacCheese Casserole
(southern style with eggs)

WHAT – a *fried-chicken dinner with collard greens and rice and candied yams and no third carb; are you kiddin' me??!!! Y'all need to come on in the house and have some this Macaroni Cheese Casserole!!!!!!!*

2 cups small elbow macaroni or small shell macaroni
1 cup half & half milk
1 cup whole milk or evaporated milk
½ stick unsalted butter
3 cups shredded 3-cheese blend
1 cup Velveeta cheese product
8 oz. brick cream cheese
1 teaspoon each - black pepper, garlic powder, yellow prepared mustard
½ teaspoon salt, ground nutmeg, dry mustard
½ teaspoon cayenne pepper
¼ cup Italian seasoned bread crumbs.
½ cup shredded 3-cheese blend

Instructions:

1. Bring macaroni to a boil and cook until al dente (careful not to overcook); then drain and set aside.

2. In a large sauce pan, heat the whole milk just short of a boil. Put in the shredded cheese, the Velveeta, and slowly stir and until all melted and you have a thick cheese sauce.
3. Now, add the half and half, the butter and 3 eggs in a separate bowl and beat; then add the brick of cream cheese. Pour in bowl with the cooled macaroni.
4. Now pour the melted and thick cheese sauce over the drained macaroni as well and stir and mix.
5. Add the pepper, garlic powder, salt and cayenne. Stir to mix.
6. Pour in 9 x 12 casserole dish.
7. Top with Italian seasoned bread crumbs and ½ cup shredded 3-cheese mix.
8. Bake 30 – 45 minutes.

Mac and Cheese
(entrée style – no eggs)

2 cups small elbow macaroni or small shell macaroni
1 cup half & half milk
1 cup whole milk or evaporated milk
½ stick unsalted butter
1 TABLEspoon olive oil
3 cups shredded 3-cheese blend
1 cup Velveeta cheese product
8 oz brick cream cheese
2 cups (cut into chunks) ham, or turkey, or chicken
½ cup celery diced
¼ cup onion minced
¼ cup button mushrooms, finely minced
1 teaspoon each black pepper, garlic powder, yellow prepared mustard
½ teaspoon salt, ground nutmeg, dry mustard
¼ cup Italian seasoned bread crumbs.
½ cup shredded 3-cheese mix

Instructions:

1. Bring macaroni to a boil and cook until al dente (careful not to overcook); then drain and set aside.
2. In a large sauce pan, heat the whole milk just short of a boil. Put in the shredded cheese, the cheez

whiz and slowly stir and until all melted and you have a thick cheese sauce. Now, add the half and half, the butter and the brick of cream cheese. Continue to stir and heat slowly until all is melted and thick.

3. Pour over drained macaroni, stir and mix.
4. Slowly sauté the celery, onion, and mushroom in 1 TABLEspoon olive oil until tender. Then add the pepper, garlic powder, salt and cayenne. Stir to mix. Add the meat chunks.
5. Pour in 9 x 12 casserole dish with the macaroni/cheese mixture – stir in to mix.
6. Top with Italian seasoned bread crumbs and ½ cup shredded 3-cheese mix.
7. Bake 30 – 45 minutes.

Collard Greens & Peppers

Good collard greens mean they must be super tender and have a good pot liquor! I remember seeing the old folks drink the pot liquor like a cup of tea, with a square of cornbread! I remember Aunt Lucille would pour it over a serving of hot cornbread in a bowl!

The trick to good greens: Do not over-season them as to overpower the natural flavor of the greens; and cook them covered, long and slow!

2 large bunches of collard greens
1 TABLEspoon of melted bacon fat
1 – 2 smoked neck bones *or* 1 – 2 smoked ham hocks *or* 1 smoked turkey wing
   (If cooking vegetarian, use 1 tablespoon of olive or vegetable oil, and omit the bacon fat, as well as the smoked meat)

2 – 3 tiny hot green peppers finely minced
1 garlic clove finely minced
1 teaspoon salt
1 teaspoon crushed red pepper flakes
1 teaspoon ground black pepper
1 TABLEspoon meat tenderizer
¼ cup granulated sugar
½ cup white vinegar
1 quart of water

Instructions:

1. Wash the greens, shake dry; then wash again and shake dry again.
2. Stack leaves, roll, and slice them in thin julienne strips.
3. In large stock pot, heat the melted bacon fat then add the garlic and slowly sauté until tender, but do not let it brown.
4. Add and bring to a boil 1 quart of the water.
5. Add the neck bones or whichever meat you're using and turn heat down to a slow boil (just a tad bit higher than a simmer).
6. Cook for 20 minutes to season the water.
7. Add the greens, salt, red pepper flakes, black pepper, meat tenderizer, granulated sugar and vinegar. Turn heat back up and bring back up to a boil.
8. Immediately turn heat down to a slow boil again, add the remaining additional water if deemed necessary.
9. Cover and simmer for 1 hour, 30 minutes.
10. Uncover and simmer an additional 30 minutes until pot liquor reduces by half, is dark green and rich.

Daddy's
Bread Pudding
(*with* Warm Bourbon Cream)

As a young child, I was never fond of bread pudding as it was just bread and raisins. But, when I watched my Daddy make bread pudding, swiping stored candied-fruits that my Mother had set aside for the early making and curing of her fruitcake, I just had to try it when he was done! One taste and I began a whole new love affair with bread pudding – it was wonderful even though he would not let me have any of the warm bourbon cream! When I make this bread pudding for a potluck group dinner, I do not use bourbon in the cream – I use a light simple syrup with rum or brandy "flavoring" instead, as some folks do not consume spirits.

When my Daddy made this bread pudding, he use to use those large disposable aluminum lasagna pans that he would get at the supermarket, as he would always have too much bread pudding for one dish!!!

Bread pudding in our family, was a way to use up old bread – nothing going to waste. I do not use a "soft" bread for bread pudding – like my Daddy, I use old stale bread. Make sure the bread is dry, hard and crusty. Cut off any mold if it has gotten onto the bread and give it enough time to soak up the wonderful custard!

Pre-heat oven at 375° - Bake 1 hour, 30 minutes at 350°

~ I ~ Emma T & Bunch

Instructions:

1. Break up a fair amount of bread in a very large bowl. If it is not dried out, let it sit all day and dry out. (Soft bead is terrible for a good bread pudding.) You should end up with the equivalent of 8 – 10 cups of chopped up bread!

2. In a mixing bowl, combine the following ingredients:
   1 cup whole milk
   1 cup buttermilk
   1 cup half & half milk
   4 whole eggs
   2 ½ cups granulated sugar
   1 TABLEspoon of cinnamon
   1 TABLEspoon of nutmeg
   ½ teaspoon of ground clove
   ¼ ground ginger
   2 TABLEspoons of vanilla extract
   Whisk this together until well blended – should look like egg nog when you're done!

3. In a second mixing bowl empty the contents of the following ingredients:
   ½ box raisins (use more if you'd like more)
   1 container of cut cubed fruitcake fruit (like Daddy, I like to use a variety of colors!)
   1 container of dried cherries for fruitcake (rough chop them)
   1 can of sliced peaches (drained and cut up a little)
   1 can of pineapple tidbits (drained)
   1 ½ cups of chopped toasted pecans for the pudding, *and also*

1 ½ cups of chopped toasted pecans for topping
1 cup light brown sugar
2 cups of warm Bourbon; or warm Rum if you prefer
Let fruit sit and soak in the liquor for about an hour. (If you do not use spirits in your cooking, use warm water with 2 TABLEspoons of dark brown sugar in it.)
Then, pour all of it over the dried bread.
(You can also add other fruits that you might like to have in your bread pudding as well. Sometimes Daddy would add shredded coconut!)

4.   Now pour the custard over the fruit, nut and bread mixture. Stir, then pour into the large lasagna pan. Let is sit for a good half-hour or so – it needs the time to soak up that wonderful custard!
Bake until done (Remember, this is a custard so a toothpick will come out clean. Another test would be to jiggle the pan to check for doneness!)
When the bread pudding comes out of the oven, you should use a large service spoon and go through the pudding once so that it is broken up a bit to receive the on-coming Warm Bourbon Cream!

5.   For the warm bourbon cream, simply take 1 stick of butter and melt it down; pour in ½ cup of bourbon and warm this on top of the stove – nicely warm; but NOT hot. Then pour in 10X sugar to give the consistency of heavy cream thickness. Pour this over the bread pudding just before serving. Sprinkle with additional 1-cup of toasted pecan pieces.

Evaporated Milk
Lemon Meringue Pie
(after the Kress Five & Dime Store)

Downtown on the square we had a Kress Five & Dime store with a lunch counter. They served the best lemon meringue pie – instead of a water base, the filing was made with milk! The taste and richness seemed to be that of evaporated can milk! As lemon pie is basically a custard pie, I've modified a lemon pie that my mother use to make by using evaporated can milk instead of water!

The Pie:
1 ½ cups sugar
½ cup of corn starch
2 cups evaporated milk
5 egg yolks
½ cup fresh-squeezed lemon juice
1 TABLEspoon fresh lemon peel zest
2 TABLEspoons butter

1 baked 9-inch "perfect" pie crust (elsewhere in this book)

Instructions:

Mix sugar, corn starch and milk in saucepan. Add beaten

egg yolks. Cook over medium heat. Watch this and constantly stir. When it become very thick, add lemon juice and lemon zest along with butter and stir until smooth. Pour into a chilled stainless steel bowl, then set aside in refrigerator to cool down for about 30 - 45 minutes. Then, pour into baked pie crust.

The Meringue:
5 egg whites
½ cup sugar
2 drops vanilla extract
1 teaspoon cream of tartar

Instructions:

Beat egg whites, vanilla and cream of tartar until soft peaks, then gradually add sugar as you continue to beat until stiff peaks. Spread over pie, making sure to seal edges. Bake at 375° until browning begins, then remove. Chill pie for at least 3 hours; but best to chill overnight!

Maple-Walnut Light Moist
Yellow Layer Cake

Watching Mother and Aunt Emma T make coconut cake, seems they took more care with the frosting than the cake! I later learned that they were making something called 7-minute frosting and you had to work quickly or the frosting would harden up on you!

One summer in New York, I had a different seven-minute frosting at one of the many coffee shops I would frequent for lunch breaks. Instead of a white frosting, it was a maple-flavored light amber frosting and covered in chopped walnuts instead of coconut. An absolutely wonderful combination that I still enjoy 40 years later! I use Aunt Emma T's light moist yellow layer cake, and frost it with this maple-flavored seven-minute frosting — it is just too wonderful! Members of our TX Kerry Blue Terrier Club loved this cake when I brought it over as my contribution to the pot luck after-the-meeting meal!

2 nine-inch light moist yellow cake layers
4 large egg whites
½ teaspoon salt
1 teaspoon cream of tartar
2 cups water
2 cups light brown sugar

Instructions:

1. In a medium-size sauce pot, bring to a hard rapid boil 2 cups of water.
2. Add the 2 cups of light brown sugar and bring back up the hard rapid boil.
3. Continue to boil until the soft-ball candy stage (See my testing hint below!).
4. In a large stand mixer, using the large bowl – whip the egg white until soft peaks.
5. Add the salt – whip a bit more to absorb the salt.
6. Add the cream of tartar – whip a bit more to absorb the cream of tartar.
7. Once sugar-syrup is ready, slowly stream it into the whipped egg whites with the mixer turned ON to a slow speed. While the mixer if accepting the hot syrup, use a rubber mixing spatula to move the frosting about the bowl to make sure all syrup is being incorporated into the whites to make the frosting!
8. Once the frosting is mixed, quickly blend in the maple flavoring.
9. Quickly frost the cake layers before the frosting becomes too difficult to use.

Mother and Aunt Emma T taught me to test soft-ball stage as follows:

a. Have a glass of water sitting on the kitchen counter.
b. Dip a teaspoon into the hot syrup and let the syrup fall off the spoon into the glass of water.

c. If the syrup clumps on the way to the bottom and clumps on the bottom, the syrup is ready.

d. At this point, you must work very quickly to incorporate the hot soft-ball sugar syrup into the egg whites in order to make the frosting!

Corn Soufflé

This is a very elegant, and rich with butter, vegetable side dish that my mother would make. The custard has a wonderful velvet texture when properly baked au bain. Served as part of an elegant dinner for company, it's like having dessert during the main course!

Cut kernels of 6 ears of fresh corn, or
2 bags of frozen organic corn - thawed *(also, drain if necessary)*

½ stick of room-temperature unsalted butter, plus another
½ stick of room-temperature unsalted butter
2 TABLEspoons of granulated sugar, *also separately*
1 cup of granulated sugar
1 cup of half & half milk
1 cup of evaporated can milk
1 TABLEspoon of vanilla
1 teaspoon each of: salt, white pepper
½ teaspoon each: dry yellow mustard, cayenne pepper
3 eggs

Instructions:

1. Grease a 9 x 13 oven-safe baking dish with ½ stick of butter.

2. Sprinkle 2 TABLEspoons of granulated sugar and coat the smeared butter in the dish.
3. Put corn kernels in dish – set aside
4. In a blender, combine – the sugar, half & half, can milk, eggs, spices, and vanilla extract.
5. Pour over corn.
6. Sit baking dish in a larger baking dish (I use my roasting pan).
7. Pour hot water in the roasting pan that it come half way up the baking dish.
8. Bake at 350° for 1 hour or until done. Custard be light brown around the edges.

Neckbones

Both Emma T and Bunch cooked their neckbones on top the stove. I use their seasonings for that great flavor; but sometimes I do my neckbones in the oven. Talk about a comfort-dinner on a fall or winter evening – neck bones is the dish! Believe me, either version with some collard greens, rice and a square of hot cornbread is a dinner that will really make ya' happy!

Emma T & Bunch method:

About 2 – 3 pounds of FRESH neckbones.
(Do <u>not</u> use smoked neck bones for this dish.)

Seasoning Mix: 1 teaspoon each blended together – salt, pepper, garlic powder, onion powder, dry mustard, cumin, cayenne

4 TABLEspoons of olive oil
2 diced onions
3 cloves garlic
1 TABLEspoon red pepper flakes
1 cup each - diced celery; diced green bell pepper
2 cups water
1 TABLEspoon Worcestershire sauce

Instructions:

1. In a stock pot, heat the olive oil then add the onions, garlic, celery and peppers and slowly sauté just until warm.
2. Add neck bones, seasoning mix, 2 cups of water, Worcestershire sauce and the red pepper flakes.
3. Bring to a boil, then turn heat down to a slow boil (just above a simmer) and cook for 1 hour and forty-five minutes (meat should be tender and ready to fall off the bones!)

Baked/braised method:

1. Pre-heat your oven to 500°.
2. In a Dutch Oven, heat the olive oil then add the onions, garlic, celery and peppers and slowly sauté just until warm.
3. Add neck bones, seasoning mix, and _only 1 cup of water_, Worcestershire sauce and red pepper flakes.
4. Bring to a boil, then cover and put in pre-heated oven. Turn down the heat to 300° and braise covered for 2 hours.

Stewed Tomatoes

These stewed tomatoes have a sweet taste to them, with a savory salty taste as well. When mother would cook them, I use to like them served over rice – especially if we were having fried chicken or fried fish. When my grandmother and her sisters cooked stewed tomatoes, they liked them over grits. Perhaps that is why my daddy also liked his stewed tomatoes over grits with some fried catfish!

About 2 – 3 pounds of fresh tomatoes
(We use small round garden-variety tomatoes – not beefsteak type!)
2 slices of salt pork (streak-o-lean)

Seasoning Mix: 1 teaspoon each – salt, pepper, garlic powder, onion powder, dry mustard, cayenne

2 diced onions
1 cloves garlic minced
1 TABLEspoon red pepper flakes
2 TABLEspoons granulated sugar
1 teaspoon white vinegar
1 TABLEspoon cornstarch
1 teaspoon Worcestershire sauce
½ cup water, *also*
1 cup water

~ I ~ Emma T & Bunch

Instructions:

1. Wash and coarse-chop the tomatoes so that you end up with large chunks. (Mother use to remove the skins first. I cook mine with the skins remaining on!) Set aside in bowl.
2. In a large hot cast-iron fry pan, slowly fry up the salt pork. Remove the pork when done.
3. Combine the Seasoning Mix, the sugar, vinegar, cornstarch and Worcestershire sauce and ½ cup of water into a savory slurry – set aside.
4. To the fry pan, add the diced onions, minced garlic and slowly sauté until tender, then add the tomato chunks and 1 cup of water and simmer for 20 minutes.
5. Add the seasoned slurry and simmer another 20 minutes. Tomatoes should be soft with a nice sauce about them.

Bunch's
Carolina Gumbo

This traditional dish is an all-time favorite of mine. It's very economical, very filling, and is a good side dish for so many main courses. I do add a touch of garlic and a bit more sugar to the recipe. You could adjust to suit your taste as well. Next time you fry fish, serve this gumbo on top a bed of fluffy white rice; add a hot square of cornbread and you're good to go!

About 2 – 3 pounds of fresh tomatoes
(We use small round garden-variety tomatoes – not beefsteak type!)
4 fresh ears of corn – slice off the kernels from the cob
8 – 10 fresh okra, sliced
2 slices of salt pork (streak-o-lean)
If cooking this as a vegetarian dish, use 2 TABLEspoons of olive oil instead of the salt pork

Seasoning Mix: 1 teaspoon each –salt, pepper, garlic powder, onion powder + dry mustard, cayenne (these are my additions to Mother's recipe)

1 medium onion, diced
1 clove garlic, minced
1 TABLEspoon red pepper flakes (this is my addition to Mother's recipe)

~ I ~ Emma T & Bunch

3 TABLEspoons granulated sugar (Mother used 2 TABLEspoons)
1 TABLEspoon cornstarch
1 cup water

Instructions:

1. Wash and coarse-chop the tomatoes so that you end up with large chunks. (Mother use to remove the skins first. I cook mine with the skins remaining on!) Set aside in bowl. Add the fresh-cut corn kernels to the bowl as well.
2. Slice the okra and set them aside in a _separate bowl!_
3. In a large hot cast-iron fry pan, slowly fry up the salt pork. Remove the pork when done _(Or heat the olive oil if vegetarian)._
4. Combine the Seasoning Mix, the sugar, vinegar, and cornstarch in the 1 cup of water into a savory slurry – set aside.
5. To the fry pan, add the diced onions, minced garlic and slowly sauté until tender, then add the tomato chunks and corn and sauté slowly for 10 minutes. Add the savory slurry and continue to simmer another 10 minutes.
6. Turn off the heat, set pan aside – then add okra and cover. (Do NOT cook any further, or else okra will become slimy!) Tomatoes should be soft with a nice sauce about them, with tender corn and nice firm al dente okra!

Emma T's Light Moist
Yellow Layer Cake

Emma T had a basic formula for moist yellow cake layers; and she passed this on to Bunch as well. Of course, mother added her extra spin to it by using a bit more extract. The basic formula is one measure of cake flour calls for half that measure for sugar and milk. For every full cup of flour, you will need 1 teaspoon of baking powder for rising, ½ cup of milk for moisture, 1 egg per cup of flour, and ½ cup of shortening to 1 cup of flour!

This is her basic yellow cake that produces three nine-inch layers. She creamed the butter and sugar before adding the egg yolks. Her technique for making her layers light and airy was to beat the egg whites into stiff peaks with cream of tartar and fold them in as the last step in making the cake batter.

She baked almost all her cakes at 350 degrees until done. Testing with a toothpick is sufficient to determine if the cake is done. Toothpick should come out clean.

This is the cake that would be used to make coconut layer cake for my sister's birthday; lemon layer cake (using lemon extract instead of vanilla) for my birthday; and yellow cake with chocolate frosting for my younger brothers' birthdays! One cake fits all she'd say to my mother!!! In essence, Aunt Emma T's layer cake was her pound cake lightened up in terms of not so much butter; not so many eggs; and aerating the batter with the egg whites!

~ I ~ Emma T & Bunch

3 cups sifted cake flour
1 ½ cups granulated sugar
1 ½ sticks unsalted butter; or ¾ cup vegetable oil
3 teaspoons baking powder
¾ teaspoons iodized table salt
3 eggs separate yolks and whites
1 teaspoon cream of tartar
1 ½ cups buttermilk *(for a sweeter cake she would use half &
half milk)*
1 tsp vanilla (mother would use 2 teaspoons)

Dorothy Jo's
Mustard Greens

The first time that I remember eating mustard greens was at Grandmother's house. She'd go across the street to her garden in the vacant lot and pick those greens so that her " precious grandchildren could have fresh greens!" Well, I just gotta tell ya' - I hated those so-called fresh greens; and when the summer was over, I never wanted to hear about a mustard green again!!!!!

Forward 20 or 30 years and we all meet up at my sister's house for Thanksgiving Dinner and lo and behold she's got mustard greens! I'm thinking, how am I gonna get out of eating these darn mustard greens! Well, I took one mouthful and was absolutely amazed. They were tender as butter and they were not bitter!

With enough prodding, I found out my sister's secret. She'll stand over that kitchen sink washing those mustards several times before taking more time forever removing each individual stem from each mustard leaf. She'll keep the stems for making a vegetable broth for soups or whatever, but that pot of greens had no stems! She also cooks her greens low and slow – seems to me a month of Sundays before those mustards are done! But, my oh my are they good!

2 large bunches of mustard greens
1 slice of hickory-smoked bacon, minced

~ I ~ Emma T & Bunch

(If cooking vegetarian, use 1 TABLEspoon of olive or vegetable oil, and omit the slice of bacon)
(Another variation is to use a smoked turkey wing as the seasoning meat! Great taste as well!)
1 teaspoon salt
2 teaspoons of granulated sugar
3 TABLEspoons white vinegar
1 quart of water

Instructions:

1. Wash the greens, shake dry; then wash again and shake dry again.
2. You really should wash them several times more – mustards are very gritty! If you don't wash them several times you're going to have that grit in the final product, and you'll end up throwing out the cooked greens from being disgusted and frustrated!
3. Take your time and remove the stems from the leaves.
4. Then, wash the mustard greens again! Really – again!
5. In large stock pot, slowly fry up the minced slice of bacon until crispy.
6. Add and bring to a boil 1 quart of the water.
7. Add the salt, sugar, vinegar – then the mustards.
8. Bring to a boil again – then immediately turn heat down to a slow boil (just a tad bit higher than a simmer).
9. Cook covered for 2 ½ hours.
10. Remove cover and continue to simmer to reduce and enrich the pot liquor!

~ II ~
The Sisters Finch

~ oOo ~

Corrie, Lucille, and Clotelle – those were three of the four whose cooking I remember rather vividly. Corrie was my daddy's mother, and she had her own special way of cooking – purely farm to table from her garden. She rarely bought food other than meat from the grocery store. To this day, I can remember sitting in the kitchen shucking dried corn to go to the local mill – half for grits; half for corn meal! My brothers and I, along with my cousins climbed the fig tree in her backyard so many times. Those figs are enjoyed today by my cousins who took a cutting from that tree and now have a fig tree in their yard. My current love of figs with goat cheese and ham developed from eating figs from that same tree!

My first taste of tiny, dark, mahogany maroon dried field peas came from my grandmother's garden that she grew on her vacant lot directly across the street from her old house. Years later, she would build a smaller house on that vacant lot where she lived the remainder of her life. Sitting around the kitchen shelling dried field peas was not a welcomed task – it took away from playtime! Eating the peas once cooked was a treat! Of course, we thought the better treat was the huckleberries and dumplings cooking on the stove top.

Aunt Lucille was grandmother's sister that still lived on the family homestead, a farm in the Kingville/Gadsden area of Richland County. Watching my Aunt Lucille hoe a row of cotton; milk a cow; feed slop to pigs/hogs; tend a garden; and make her wonderful straight-from-the-garden tomato/onion soup amazed me as a youngster. Until those wonderful summer weeks spent on my great grand-parent's farm, I never knew there was a tomato soup that did not come from a can! I learned later in life that Aunt Lucille was a diabetic and her penchant for fresh food from the garden was a great weapon against the symptoms of the disease!

I think the older sisters impart the cooking skills to the younger ones. It surely seemed so spending a summer living with my Aunt Clotelle at the end of a college year. Her cooking was southern food with a Bronx twist! To this day, I always try and duplicate her sweet potato pie – the most perfect I've ever eaten. Bus trips with church families to Asbury Park was a highlight when daughter Pat would make a watermelon salad of fresh fruits! I now do a similar salad and have added a coconut cream dressing as a side condiment to make it a dessert of fresh fruits! Pondering memories of wonderful meals at Aunt Clotelle and Uncle Henry's house, I find myself looking at an old photograph of a holiday dinner. One of the highlights of that dinner was the presence of our cousin Estelle and her husband Richard. Dinner would end with Cousin Estelle's fresh coconut cake made with fresh coconut milk as one of the desserts; along with Aunt Clotelle's sweet potato pie of course! Both were divine poetry for the palate!

During the Florida years growing up with my two

brothers, my Daddy's big thing on Saturday was taking his three sons fishing for largemouth bass on Lake Eloise in Winter Haven, FL, or putting in at Long Boat Key outside Sarasota to go out for blues! Of course, my youngest brother being about second or third grade at the time, it seems to have never failed that as soon as we got out on the water he would let Daddy know he had to go! Daddy's solution was a portable pot of sorts to take care that little constant interruption!

Catfish Stew was a specialty that my Daddy was known for making upon quite a bit of demand from family members. A bowl of it with a square of cornbread and an ice-cold beer was a treat that he and my adult aunts, uncles and cousins really enjoyed! As a young fella, having a catfish stare at me while using pliers to help remove skin during the dressing phase was not a task that endeared me to eating it later! Not to worry, my Daddy had another fish dish that I could never get my fill of – Stuffed largemouth bass! This was a treat that my daddy taught me to make on the BBQ grill; but, I also find that it can be made very well when broiled in the oven during times when outside weather is a deterrent for grilling!

Saturday nights of fresh-caught fish would sometimes be the result of a mess of bream, crappie or bluegill. My mother would fry those up with her Carolina Gumbo (i.e., okra, tomato and corn) that would be an appropriate and mighty delicious topping for her fluffy white rice, or as my Daddy liked it, over some grits! That, with a square of cornbread was a Saturday-night fish fry that was some *"shonuff good eatin'"*!

Hoppin' John

I loved the way we had Hoppin' John. Everybody used very tiny, dark mahogany-colored dried field peas! My Grandmother's Hoppin' John was really good, and this is her way of making it.

1 small bag of tiny field peas
½ cup water
1 slice fat back, *or*
1 smoked neck bone

Seasoning Mix:
1 teaspoon each - salt, pepper, garlic powder, onion powder

1 small onion, diced
1 clove garlic, finely minced
3 cups water
1 cup uncooked long-grain rice

Instructions:

1. In a hot sauce pot, add the fatback and ½ cup of water and slowly bring to a boil.
2. Pour off the water, then continue to cook on very low heat until fat back is light brown, the skin on it

is crisp and there's a TABLEspoon of bacon fat in the pot. Removed the cooked fat back!

3. Add the field peas and sauté on low heat until coated with the bacon fat

4. Add 2 cups of water, bring to a rapid boil – then reduce heat, cover and simmer the peas for 1 hour until tender.

5. Then, add 1 cup of long-grain rice, 1 more cup of water, and continue to simmer for another 20 minutes or until rice is done and tender. *(Do not overcook the rice. As soon as you see a faint line on the middle of the rice gain, completely turn off the heat and let the steam finish the rice!)*

Aunt Lucille's
Johnny Ho Corn Cakes

Early Sunday morning at my great grand parents farm, Aunt Lucille made sure we were awaken for Sunday School with the house filled with gospel music. One of her recordings of either Sister Rosetta Thorpe, or Edna Gallman Cook or Mahaliah Jackson would be on the record player! Sunday morning breakfast was like all other mornings – food she grew and meat she raised and had slaughtered, cooking it all from scratch!

Her treat for us on Sunday must have been a Finch tradition, because my Grand Mother Corrie had the same Sunday morning breakfast treat when we visited with her – Johnny Ho Corn Cakes with a thick syrup from a can with a little boy pictured on the label, along with strips of thick bacon or homemade sausage!

They both would cook the bacon first and use the bacon drippings as the fat for the corn cake batter! I've modernized the recipe a bit by using vegetable oil.

In a medium-size bowl, mix into a batter:
2 cups Yellow corn meal
½ cup All-purpose flour
1 teaspoon baking powder
½ teaspoon baking soda
1 TABLEspoon sugar
3 TABLEspoons vegetable oil

~ II ~ The Sisters Finch

1 egg
½ cup Whole buttermilk
½ cup water

Instructions:

1. *Grease and heat large cast-iron fry pan*
2. *Using large serving spoon, pour pancake-size corn cakes! When bubbles/open holes show, flip and finish cooking!*
3. *Serve with thick country-style syrup!*

The Sisters Finch
Homestead Corn Bread

This is the cornbread that Aunt Lucille and Grandmother would make in a quick minute! It's a typical country-style savory-corn-sweet type of cornbread. These days, when I make it, I also add 2 tablespoons of sugar; 1 teaspoon of vanilla; and 3 tablespoons of mayonnaise. This gives the cornbread a sweeter flavor and nicer crumb when I'm doing the various muffins noted below.

2 cups yellow corn meal
1 cup all-purpose flour
2 teaspoons baking powder
1 teaspoon baking soda
¼ teaspoon iodized table salt
⅓ cup melted pork fat *(use vegetable oil instead if you like)*
1 cup WHOLE buttermilk *(use low fat instead if you like)*
2 large eggs

Instructions:

1. Everything in the mixing bowl at once
2. Beat slowly until just blended
3. Pour into 9 x 12 buttered or oiled/greased pan
4. Bake at 425° until golden brown

~ II ~ The Sisters Finch

__I also use this batter for__:
Mexican-style cornbread with corn kernels, diced tri-color bell peppers, diced onions, diced jalapeno peppers. I also use a sweet version when making various muffins such as blueberry, cranberry, raisin & pecan, dried mixed fruit.

__For a pan of cornbread dressing; of stuffing for pork chops, I use this recipe.__
(I crumble it; add diced onion, celery, multi-color bell peppers, spices [salt, pepper, garlic powder, onion powder, sage, thyme, cayenne, Turmeric], eggs, milk and broth. Stir/blend, pour into greased baking pan, bake again at 425° until golden brown, but still moist!)

Aunt Lucille's
Beef Veggie Soup

Spending a few weeks on my great grandparents farm/ homestead with my Aunt Lucille provided many a lessons of "waste-not"! This is a soup that she would make with vegetables from the garden. (I use some fresh vegetables, and supplement them with a bag of frozen mixed vegetables as well.) Her vegetable soup would be very hearty with lots of beef. She could put lots of meat in it and still be very frugal because she would use beef neckbones. Very meaty – very cheap; and when simmered for a long cooking time – also very tender!

2 pounds beef neckbones
⅓ cup olive oil
1 teaspoon each – salt, pepper, garlic powder, onion powder
4 cups water
3 large Russet white potatoes, peeled and cut into chunks
12 small boiling onions
4 large carrots – peeled and cut into chunks
2 stalks celery, cut into chunks
1 pound bag frozen mixed vegetables
10 medium tomatoes, diced
2 cups tomato puree

~ II ~ The Sisters Finch

Instructions:

1. In a large stock pot heat olive oil and add neck bones. Cook on high heat for 3 minutes to give them a bit of a browning. Add the salt, pepper, onion powder, water and simmer for medium-low heat for 45 minutes.
2. Then add the potatoes and carrots and simmer an additional 45 minutes.
3. Then add all remaining ingredients and continue to simmer for 1 hour.
4. Turn off heat and leave covered for 30 minutes before serving.

Aunt Lucille's
Tomato ~ Onion Soup

Until I saw my aunt make this soup, as a young child I was certain that all tomato soup came in a can! This fresh tomato soup is really good! I would eat several bowls of it with a wedge of her Johnny Ho Cake iron-skillet cornbread!

2 pounds medium-size garden tomatoes, diced
1 pound yellow sweet onions, thick sliced and chopped
1 strip streak-o-lean salt pork
6 cups water
3 chicken backs, or 6 chicken necks
1 teaspoon each salt, pepper, garlic powder, onion powder
1 TABLEspoon granulated sugar
1 teaspoon white vinegar
¼ cups cornstarch

Instructions:

1. In a large stock pot cook the salt pork and remove it from the pot, leaving the rendered fat. Then, add the chicken backs and brown them.
2. Add 1 cup of water, cover and boil the chicken backs until tender. Then remove the backs from the pot, leaving the stock.

3.   Add 5 cups of water and all the remaining ingredients. Cover and simmer on medium-low heat for 1 hour.
4.   Remove from heat; remain covered and allow to cool off a bit before serving.

Tip: This soup is also very good with cooked rice added just before serving.

Daddy's Stuffed
Largemouth Bass

My best memories of bass fishing with my Daddy and two brothers were the days we spent on Lake Eloise in Winter Haven, FL. We use to watch the Cypress Gardens ski show from the boat while Daddy would troll the lake. Suddenly a strike, and what excitement – those bass were monster size and one could feed us all for dinner!

Daddy would fire up the grill, stuff the bass and cook it outside. I find that this fish does just as well inside the oven under the broiler when the weather is not good for being outside to use the grill My brother Brownie also used stripped bass, as it is a firm-flesh fish and is great for broiling. You will find this recipe suitable for grouper and snapper as well.

This recipe will feed 6 people only needing a baked potato and salad as sides.

1 large, (8 – 10 pounds) largemouth or stripped bass
(leave whole with butterfly dress)
1 TABLEspoon olive oil
1 large sliced beefsteak tomato
1 large white onion
(a yellow onion will be too sweet)
1 cup sliced button mushrooms
1 large lemon sliced with skin on
1 large yellow banana squash

~ II ~ The Sisters Finch

1 large green zucchini squash low corn
¼ cup fresh lemon juice
1 teaspoon each salt, pepper, garlic powder
1 TABLEspoon lemon zest

Instructions:

1. Put fish on heavy-duty aluminum foil.
2. Stuff fish with sliced vegetables and sprinkle with half the seasoning.
3. Pour the lemon juice in the cavity as well and close the fish.
4. Brush top of fish with olive oil and sprinkle the remaining seasoning on it.
5. *If using an outside grill,* put fish on grill – do NOT close up the foil – smoke on low flame closed-grill until done – about 45 minutes to 1 hour.
6. *If using broiler inside oven* – do NOT close up the foil – broil on low heat until done – about 30 minutes.

Daddy's Catfish Stew
Carolina Bouillabaisse

I never hear people talk about, nor do I see Catfish Stew being made or served these days! During my growing-up years in the late 50s and early 60s, my Daddy would get requests to make his Catfish Stew! Helping him dress out a catfish did not endear me to it — couldn't get past that look of a catfish staring at me as I'm taking a pair of pliers removing the skin!!!!! I call his Catfish Stew, a sort of Carolina Bouillabaisse!

1 large, (6 - 8 pounds) catfish, dressed and cut into chunks *(this should yield 1 ½ – 2 pounds of catfish meat)*
2 TABLEspoons olive oil
1 clove garlic, coarsely minced
1 large coarsely diced/chopped onion
4 stalks medium-diced celery
2 large coarsely diced bell pepper
3 large russet potatoes, diced large chunks
1 cup sliced button mushrooms
6 – 8 peeled medium-diced garden tomatoes
2 quarts chicken broth
1 large can (24 oz) tomato puree
1 TABLEspoon each salt, pepper, paprika, cayenne pepper

Instructions:

~ II ~ The Sisters Finch

1. Heat stock pot to hot; then add olive oil and turn heat down to medium.
2. Add garlic and onion and slowly sauté until tender – do not brown
3. Add celery, peppers, mushroom and continue to sauté for 10 minutes
4. Add potatoes, tomatoes, chicken broth cover and simmer until the potatoes are fork-tender done
5. Add tomato puree and spices and the catfish and simmer for 15 minutes
6. Turn off heat and let stew rest (covered) for 20 minutes before serving

Grandmother Corrie's
Buttermilk Pie

What I call a buttermilk pie is something that my grandmother made from sour milk in the fridge. She would pour off the whey, and whip up the remaining sour-milk-cheese in a quick minute with eggs, sugar, vanilla and a tad bit of flour! She and Aunt Lucille did not let anything go to waste! Sour milk was good for biscuits, cornbread, as well as this pie.

I use whole buttermilk when making this pie. It can be made with a low-fat buttermilk as well. I also do a variation on this pie with a coconut-pecan topping that I call a Buttermilk Crunch Pie shown elsewhere in this cookbook!

4 egg yolks
4 egg whites (beaten stiff)
½ cup melted butter
1 teaspoon vanilla extract
1 teaspoon butter flavor
4 cups whole buttermilk
3 cups granulated sugar
¼ cup all-purpose flour (for a creamier texture, omit the flour!)
2 9-inch pie crusts

Instructions:

I mix everything except the whites all at one time. When

~ II ~ The Sisters Finch

well mixed, I then fold in the stiff egg white. Then I pour everything into the pie crust and bake slowly on 325. When I see brown rims and the pies no longer jiggle when slightly shaken, I know that they are done. You can also use the toothpick method to test if they are done. Toothpick should come out clean! Once done, I leave them out for at least 2 hours to cool at room temperature.

~ III ~
Fly Away Home

~ oOo ~

The experience of eating so many dishes from so many wonderful cooks keeps one ever cognizant of good food no matter one's location. Such was definitely the case with this author while traveling on business and pleasure during the early years of a professional career.

Noting similarities of food and its preparation from region to region and country to country confirms the notion that we are more alike than different! One region's Corn Cakes are the same as may be termed in another region as Johnny Ho Cake! One country's plum pudding when baked instead of steamed, may be another country's fruit cake with some additions!

As we grow and our taste is enhanced with additional knowledge of food, we take liberties with ingredients; change techniques; and may come up with new dishes in our own kitchens at home. I've taken the liberty of sharing some of mine with you in this part of the book.

It seems that the farther away one gets, the closer one gets home while away at a distant place! Reminiscing of my first real trip away from home, I think of my dear Cousin Willie Mae who was Aunt Minnie Mae's daughter. I had just finished high school and wanted to run off to New York to work for the summer before entering my first year of college. I think I picked New York because my sister was born there; my father did his graduate degree there; and I had always heard about the magic and vitality of the city! On the other hand, my mother was very concerned about her 17-year-old son going off to the Big City alone, though I had aunts, uncles and cousins there. So, my cousin Willie Mae said I would stay with her family that first summer which would allow her and her husband Courtenay to teach me how to get around and how to be safe in the city!

Willie Mae was a French major in college; and a bit of the dramatics and comedy of theatrics of the romance of foreign languages was part of her personality as well! Though I had not seen her for many years, once I arrived in New York and see her coax her 8 year-old daughter Nikki to stop with the dramatics of a small tantrum to get her way about something, it was evident that she was my mother's niece; that her mother was definitely one of the older siblings of my mother!

My cousin made a Sunday dinner that was one pot, on top of the stove that was so good I could never forget it. She took a Boston Butt piece of pork, braised it on the stove top with onions, carrots, celery and some seasoning. She also had a pot of fluffy white rice next to it! My goodness, I never ate so well! Of course, the preparation of the meal was interrupted by Nikki's demand for constant attention! To her dissatisfaction, she was not getting the amount of attention that she determined was necessary to keep her quiet so she began a small dramatic performance commonly known as a temper tantrum! Not to be dissuaded, Willie Mae's immediate reaction: "Nikki please, they have already given out the Oscars for this year!!!!!!!!"

~ III ~ Fly Away Home

To this day, I cook Willie Mae's braised pork meal on occasion and always have such wonderful loving memories of her. I call this dish "Willie Mae's Bronx One Pot" in honor of that apartment on Westchester Avenue, which doors were open to me for my very first summer away from home.

I find myself cooking more and more with wines and spirits as I experiment. I am reminded of my daddy's saying when he used spirits in some of his dishes: "If it's not good enough for me to drink; it's not good enough to go into my food!" I have found that to be a real pearl of wisdom when setting up my bar at home as well as using wines and spirits in my cooking.

Growing up, I remember the rare occasion of having lamb chops or a piece of roasted lamb served with some mint jelly! Once I moved to New York City, I experienced lamb with a rather sophisticated mint sauce that I enjoy to this day. Traveling to Ireland was the ultimate experience for eating Lamb Stew – an ambrosia of meat and vegetables that I find as mouthwatering as any stew I have ever eaten. I do add a bit of stout to my lamb stew – I think you might enjoy the results of this enhancement!

Fruits can be such an treat when used for seasoning and accompanying meat dishes. So much so, that many times I will use them as the major side dish or sometimes the only side dish for an entrée! Immediately, apricots come to mind with venison chops with a bit of apricot brandy to deglaze after the initial sauté! I have some hunting buddies that love this way of preparing their bounty from a weekend of hunting! Fresh oranges are great for glazing and serving with roasted duck using some orange liqueur to assist with the saucing!

Cranberries and pecans in a rice dish to serve with Cornish hens takes the place of any stuffing and is an elegant presentation for those tender small birds!

Taking liberties with childhood desserts has been a bit of a game for me! It still gives me great pleasure to pick a fully-ripened peach from a tree. Of course, in addition to having it as a snack, I do a few things with fresh peaches beyond my mother's fresh peach cobbler! Topping a peach with a little of my Bourbon Cream and butter-roasted chopped pecans gives you my Broiled Peaches deLeon, a quick and impressive dessert served in a sherbet dish! Fresh peaches poached in a spiced simple syrup that I call Peaches Vera! With either one of these, you'll find that you've scored game points with dinner guests!

Farmers' markets and large sophisticated grocers know that today's consumer appreciates fresh fruit all year long and have secured sources to supply such demand. A cocktail of fresh berries with a brandied sour cream is a terrific Berries Romanoff that takes the classic dessert a step farther in its offering!

I'm getting hungry – let's cook somethin'!

Turkey Wings Margo
(with Baking Dust!)

When I created this recipe, I just wanted to make sure I had some gravy for my rice and not have to also put on another pot to cook vegetables! I passed this recipe on to my friend Margo who consented to cook several of my recipes. When she cooked this dish, she quickly told me how perfect these wings were and that her husband Clay requested that she always cook turkey wings this way! I was so happy with her report, I named the dish in her honor! So, next time you see Margo Moorer, the actress, in the movie Forest Gump, you will know that she can also throw down on some Turkey Wings Margo! And, you will know for whom the recipe/dish is named!

These are tender, fall-off-the-bone flavorful turkey wings with their own smooth seasoned sauce!

3 fresh turkey wings separate drum stick and flat
(set tips aside and freeze for making stock at another time)
1 cup each diced celery, onion, bell pepper, shredded carrots

Instructions:

1. In glass casserole pan (at least 9 x 12) lay out the wings.
2. Sprinkle very heavy with Yard Bird Dust

3. Add 1 cup water in bottom of pan.
4. Add diced celery, onions, bell peppers and shredded carrots.
5. Bake "uncovered" for 20 minutes on 500 degrees.
6. Slide pan out from the oven; cover with foil; return to oven and bake covered at 225° for 2 hours!

Roast Chicken
(with Plum Chutney)

This is a very moist and flavorful roast chicken. During late summer when fruits are plentiful, I take advantage of the opportunity to serve it with a chilled and spicy plum chutney.

Pre-heat oven to 500° - Roast bird at 400°.

1 medium-size chicken (quartered)
1 TABLEspoon unsalted butter, melted

Season with 1 teaspoon each of salt, white pepper, tarragon and dried thyme leaves.

¼ cup water

Instructions:

1. Wash the bird and dry by sitting on paper towels.
2. Elevate bird on a meat rack; set rack on a cookie pan and refrigerate uncovered overnight.
3. In a 9 x 12-inch baking dish, add ¼ cup water
4. Brush the melted butter or bacon fat on the quartered chicken; sprinkle with the seasoning.
5. Roast the bird UNcovered for 1 hour – skin should be crisp, golden brown.

6. Remove bird from oven and let rest for 10 minutes.
7. Serve with chilled plum chutney.

~ III ~ Fly Away Home

Mango-Peach
Plum Chutney

2 TABLEspoons olive oil
1 each – medium and finely chopped
red onion, white onion, yellow onion, and jalapeno chili
pepper
12-14 assorted plums, (about 2 pounds), halved, pitted,
and cut into large chunks
2-3 ripe peaches, haled, pitted and cut into ½-inch pieces
6 dried mangoes – chopped
⅓ cup packed light-brown sugar
⅔ cup packed white granulated
4 TABLEspoons cider vinegar
1 ½ teaspoon curry powder
½ teaspoon ground ginger
1 TABLEspoon Dijon mustard
½ teaspoon cinnamon
½ teaspoon nutmeg
½ teaspoon red pepper flakes
½ teaspoon cayenne pepper
1 cup water
¼ cup cream sherry or Marsala wine

Instructions:

Heat skillet – then add 1 TABLEspoon oil, onion, and

jalapeno; cook until softened, about 3 minutes. Increase heat to medium-high; add plums, mangoes, peaches, sugar, vinegar, curry powder, ginger, and ½ cup water. Bring to a boil; reduce to a simmer, and cook until plums and mangoes are softened and liquid is slightly syrupy, about 30 minutes. The peaches will soften earlier and be a part of the thickened sauce for the plums and mangoes! I usually keep a couple of quart-size Mason jars on hand to store this chutney in the fridge! If you know how to can, it will do well as part of your preserved stock in your pantry!

Hardwood Ham
(with Jamaican Rum Glaze)

The Jamaican Rum Glaze really puts this ham on a different plane! Slice it thin and put additional glaze on the slices as a sauce. Absolutely delicious for a late-supper after a fox hunt or fishing trip!

Pre-heat oven at: 500°
Bake covered at 350° for 1 hour, 30 minutes
or more dependent upon the size of the ham.

Glaze then continue to bake uncovered at 250° for 30 minutes.

This recipe calls for **a whole hardwood smoked ham** with skin intact. You can also do this with a smoked, salty country ham–you would need to soak it in water.

For the Spice Mix:
4 TABLEspoons each of –
salt, pepper, paprika, dried orange peel, dry mustard powder

For the Glaze:
1 cup light brown sugar
½ cup granulated sugar

¼ cup apple cider vinegar
1 cup dark Jamaican Rum
½ cup frozen orange juice concentrate
½ cup water
¼ cup cornstarch
¼ spice mix above

Season the ham:
1. If you are using a "country ham", you will need to immerse the ham in water for at least 4 hours. If you are using a hardwood smoked ham, you should move on to the next step of removing the skin!
2. Carefully remove skin from the ham, then score fat in a diamond pattern.
3. Sprinkle ¾ of the seasoning mix liberally on all sides of the ham. Then, refrigerate the ham for at least 4 hours; preferably overnight.
4. Save the remaining ¼ of the seasoning mix to make the glaze.

Make the glaze:
In a sauce pot combine all glaze ingredients and simmer until thickened. Then set aside to cool to be used after the ham bakes!

To bake the ham:
5. Sit the seasoned ham on a rack in a roasting pan. Add 1 cup of apple pineapple juice and 1 cup of water in the pan. Cover and bake the ham covered for one hour and thirty minutes; more dependent upon size of ham.

~ III ~ Fly Away Home

6. Remove the ham from the oven, uncover and let it rest for 20 minutes.
7. Brush the glaze on the ham liberally! Then return the ham to the oven and let it continue to bake uncovered at 250° for 30 minutes.
8. Remove the glazed ham from the oven and let it rest at least 30 minutes before slicing.

Willie Mae's
Bronx One Pot

My cousin Willie Mae lived in Bronx, NY and it was my first summer away from home. This is what she made one Sunday for dinner. It was the first time I had seen a Boston Butt cooked on top the stove. This dish is a pork pot roast of sorts, braised to perfection on the stove top with some vegetables and just enough seasoning dust to make its owns sauce.

When comfort food is the goal; when hearty substantial eating without a lot of preparation fussing about is the goal; when a gracious plenty at a very economical outlay is the goal – then my cousin Willie Mae's Bronx One Pot Dinner is the entrée! The only accompaniment she'd have was a serving dish of fluffy steamed white rice. Oh my goodness – I could have this for dinner right now!

This recipe will serve 6 to 8 very hungry dinner guest, and you will still have leftover for sliced pork sandwiches a couple days later!

1 large Boston Butt pork roast
2 TABLEspoons olive oil
3 cloves finely minced fresh garlic
1 teaspoon each salt, pepper
2 TABLEspoons all-purpose flour
3 large carrots, peeled and sliced
2 stalks celery, peeled and sliced

~ III ~ Fly Away Home

2 medium white onions, quartered
2 large Russet white potatoes
(peeled and diced into medium chunks)
3 cups water

Instructions:

1. Heat a Dutch Oven pot until hot; then add the 2
    TABLEspoons of olive oil. Then, turn down heat
    and add the minced garlic and sauté slowly on the
    medium heat until soft (Do not let the garlic
    brown.).
2. Combine the salt, pepper and flour in a small bowl
    and rub it on the fresh Boston Butt and let it rest for
    10 minutes or so.
3. Add the Boston Butt to the pot and continue to
    cook uncovered until slightly browned. Then, add
    the carrots, celery, onions and potatoes and 3 cups
    of water. Cover and simmer on stove top for 1 ½
    hours on low heat. Then fork test the meat – it
    should be very tender.
4. Uncover and continue to simmer for 20 minutes to
    reduce the sauce to thicken it just a bit.
5. Remove from stove, cover and let the dish rest for
    20 minutes before serving.
6. To serve, place Boston Butt on cutting board and
    allow to cool down for another 20 minutes. Then
    slice with an electric knife for consistent, clean
    serving slices.
7. If sauce is not thick enough, now is the time to add
    2 additional TABLEspoons of all-purpose flour to 3
    or 4 spoonfuls of the cooking liquid, stir into a

smooth slurry, pour it back into the pot and simmer until desired thickness of sauce is accomplished. (You may desire to add additional seasoning at this point.)

Got leftovers? – Of course you do!

Sliced Pork Sandwich

2 slices of whole wheat bread,
or your favorite bread
(cinnamon-raisin is a good choice too!)
spread a TABLEspoon of Dijon mustard on each slice
add a pineapple ring on one slice
3 slices of the leftover pork
1 thin slice of red onion
1 dried apricot half
1 dried apple ring

Berries Romanoff

Very few things are as wonderful as fresh fruit. This medley of fresh fruit is quite the sophisticated adult parfait; yet very easy to make. This take on the classic strawberry dessert includes the strawberry, but also adds blackberries, blueberries and raspberries to make it a wonderful fruit medley. The spirited syrup and Romanoff Cream makes it an "adults only" treat that's quite impressive for last minute unexpected dinner guests!

1 cup each –
fresh strawberries
blackberries
blueberries
raspberries

Spiked simple syrup:
½ cup water
¼ cup granulated sugar
3 TABLEspoons VSOP cognac

Romanoff Cream:
2 cups sour cream
¼ cup dark brown sugar
¼ cup Courvoisier VSOP
Blend with hand whisk – let sit in fridge overnight for flavors to meld

Instructions:

1. Bring ½ cup water to a rapid boil, then remove from heat. Pour into small bowl; and stir in and dissolve ¼ cup granulated sugar. Let syrup cool a bit, then stir in 3 TABLEspoons of VSOP cognac. Then put in refrigerator to completely cool.
2. In a separate small bowl, with a hand whisk blend the sour cream, dark brown sugar and the ¼ cup of VSOP cognac. Cover and chill until cold.
3. Wash the fruit; then drain on a paper towel to dry.
4. In a medium-size bowl add fruit and spiked simple syrup; toss lightly. Put in fridge to chill! *(Not too cold or you'll ruin them!!!)*
5. To serve: Spoon macerated fruit into footed goblets. *(Do NOT include the syrup);* spoon liberal dollops of Romanoff Cream over them!

Bourbon Custard
Buttered Pecan Ice Cream

(I use an old-fashion electric pine bucket model ice cream machine. The Bourbon "Custard" is not an egg and milk traditional custard, but rather a thick clear sauce to ripple through the ice cream. This is an "adult" dessert. For the younger diner, omit the "Bourbon Custard"!!!)

1. **Slowly bring to a simmering boil**
   1 ½ cups heavy cream
   2 cups half & half milk
   4 cups whole milk

Once hot,

2. **add and dissolve**
   1 cup granulated white sugar
   ½ cup dark brown sugar
   ½ cup light brown sugar
   1 stick (½ cup) unsalted butter
   1 TABLEspoon of Mexican Vanilla extract

3. **Stir until all is smooth** –set aside and let cool down a bit – then, pour contents into bowl of ice cream maker; churn according to instructions. When semi-soft ice cream forms,

add,

4. 3 ½ cups of chopped pecans and continue to churn until there are nuts through out.

Then,

5. Pour in the Bourbon "custard" to get a swirl/ripple throughout the ice cream!
6. Pour or paddle the finished ice cream into disposable plastic square dishes with the lid. (This is what I use to freeze my ice cream. I use the ½-gallon size square dishes with the blue plastic top.)

Bourbon Custard:
Bring to a boil, then turn down and simmer until thick.

¾ cup water * 4 TABLEspoons cornstarch * ½ cup light brown sugar * ½ cup good Bourbon whiskey

White Chocolate
Walnut Ice Cream

(Note: I use the old-fashion electric pine bucket model ice cream machine.)

1. **Slowly bring to a simmering bowl**
   1 ½ cups heavy cream
   2 cups half & half
   4 cups whole milk

Once hot,

2. **add and dissolve**
   3 cups granulated white sugar
   3 ½ cups grated white chocolate
   1 TABLEspoon Mexican Vanilla extract

Stir until all is smooth –set aside and let cool down a bit.

Then,

4. Pour contents into bowl of ice cream maker; churn according to instructions. When semi-soft ice cream forms, add the walnuts.
5. Pour or paddle into a disposable plastic square dishes with the lid. (This is what I use to freeze my ice cream. I use the ½-gallon size square dishes with the blue plastic top.)

Bourbon Yogurt Cream

I originally created this spirited topping to use as a dollop on a slice of my Apple Oatmeal Upside-Down Cake! It is also nice on a slice of pecan pie or a serving of a warm fruit cobbler!

2 cups plain Greek yogurt
¼ cup dark brown sugar
¼ cup good Bourbon whiskey

Instructions:

1. Blend with hand whisk chill overnight for flavors to meld
2. Spoon over pound cakes, fruit cobblers, etc.

Bourbon Cream deLeon

This is a light whipped cream that is quite spirited for an adult topping on fruit desserts such as my Broiled Peaches!

1 cup heavy whipping cream
3 TABLEspoons 10X confectioners' sugar
3 TABLEspoons good-quality Bourbon whiskey

Instructions:

1. Whip cream until soft peaks; then gradually add sugar as you continue to whip into stiff peaks.
2. With mixer turned off, use hand whisk and blend in the 3 TABLEspoon of Bourbon whiskey.
3. Chill overnight in refrigerator.

Coconut Cream Dressing

My cousin would make a watermelon salad for family outings during the summer months. Many years later, I would make that watermelon salad to take to potluck gatherings during summer months. Once the watermelon is carved and the flesh is scooped out, cut into chunks and combined with other seasonal fruits, the presentation is quite spectacular.

To enhance the fruit and make it a wonderful dessert, I created this coconut cream dressing to be poured over individual servings of the salad. As no sugar is added to the fruit, this sweet creamy dressing is just the right amount of additional sweetness that is an enhancement! With two shortbread cookies, it is a complete dessert course!

2 cups sour cream
3 TABLEspoons – 10X confectioners' sugar
¼ cup - coconut milk
½ cup – half & half milk
1 teaspoon coconut flavoring
¼ cup finely ground coconut flakes

Instructions:

Put all ingredients in a blender and process for 2 minutes.

~ III ~ Fly Away Home

Upside-Down
Apple Walnut Cake

This is a bit of a take on my mother's layer cake that she would use to make pineapple upside-down cake. My little quirks to her cake are the use of apples as the fruit with walnuts added as well for crunch! I season the apples as though I was going to make an old-fashion American apple pie. For the cake to be a little rustic, I substitute ½ of her flour with a made-up oatmeal flour. The cake is still light and tender, though with a nice rustic taste to compliment the walnuts. I serve this with a dollop of my Bourbon Yogurt Cream or the Bourbon Cream deLeon on top for a spirited dessert by a fireplace of a cool fall night!

For the Upside-down:
½ cup unsalted butter, melted
2 medium tart apples, peeled, cored and medium-sliced
wedges
1 cup walnuts, coarsely chopped

Seasoning Mix:
1 cup granulated sugar
2 TABLEspoons cornstarch
1 teaspoon each cinnamon, nutmeg, ground cloves,
ground ginger
½ teaspoon fresh lemon zest

For the cake:
Mix altogether at one time!
1 cup granulated sugar
½ cup unsalted butter
2 large eggs
1 cup whole buttermilk
1 TABLEspoon vanilla extract
½ teaspoon table salt, iodized
1 cup oatmeal flour
(To make this flour, put old-fashion oats in food processor and process until of coarse corn-meal texture.)
1 cup All-purpose flour
1 teaspoon baking powder

Instructions:

1. Pour melted butter in 10-inch x 2-inch cake pan.
2. Sprinkle chopped walnuts in the buttered pan.
3. In a medium-size bowl, stir apples and seasoning mix until all apples are well coated.
4. Carefully arrange seasoned apples in a cake pan overlapping so that bottom of pan is covered with all the apples.
5. Carefully pour the cake batter so as not to disturb the apples.
6. Bake at 350 for 45 minutes to an hour; or until cake is done. Test with toothpick.
7. Let cool in pan for 30 minutes, then with a cake plate on top, invert and let cake fall onto cake plate.

Brown Sugar
Buttermilk Pound Cake

This is a variation of my Aunt Emma T's all-butter pound cake!
I take a few liberties – brown sugar; pecans; buttermilk!

Preheat oven: 350° – Bake at 350°
Use full-size round tube pound cake/angel cake pan

2 ½ cups dark brown sugar
1 cup granulated white sugar
4 cups sifted cake flour
1 cup ground pecan flour
(I measure 2 cups of roasted pecans in the food processor and grind into a cup of pecan flour)

½ teaspoon salt
1 teaspoon baking powder
1 cup chopped pecans
3 sticks of unsalted butter
6 large eggs
1 teaspoon pure vanilla extract
1 teaspoon butter & nut flavoring
Buttermilk glaze (See recipe in No. 5 below)

Instructions:

1. Put sugars and butter in large mixing bowl; beat on slow speed until incorporated. Then beat on high speed until creaming is completely done – should be very fluffy!
2. Slow mixer down and add one egg at the time, until all eggs are incorporated. Then, beat on high speed until creaming is completely done again! Should be fluffy again, but more like soufflé or custard texture. Add the flavorings and use "stir" speed to blend into the sugar, butter, egg mixture!
3. Sift together the sifted flour; pecan flour; salt and baking powder. Add all of the dry ingredients at once to the sugar, butter, egg and flavorings creamed mixture. Blend in using the "stir" speed. While blending, add the buttermilk little by little until all is used.
4. Bake until done. Let cool completely in pan (i.e., maybe 2 hours or so) with a moist towel over the pan. When cooled, invert onto cake plate.
5. Make buttermilk glaze (1 stick butter melted; 2 cups 10X Confectioners' sugar; ½ cup buttermilk; 1 teaspoon of vanilla; ½ cup of melted brown sugar). Drizzle on top of cake and garnish with chopped pecans.

~ III ~ Fly Away Home

Lemon Cream
Pound Cake

When I make this, I freeze half the batter for a second cake at a later date. If being used for family gatherings, I use all the batter and make two cakes in large pound-cake tube pans (angel-cake pans). This cake has a very fine crumb, and I use a buttermilk-type margarine which gives this cake an extra tart zing to compliment the fresh lemon zest!

2 sticks of unsalted butter
4 sticks of buttermilk margarine
2 bricks (8 ounces each) cream cheese
12 eggs
2 TABLEspoons lemon extract
2 TABLEspoon fresh lemon zest
6 cups cake flour
6 cups granulated sugar

Instructions:

1. Cream the butter, margarine and cream cheese until fluffy.
2. Add the sugar and continue to cream until fluffy again.
3. Add the eggs 2 or 3 at the time and whip until fluffy.

4. Add the extract; blend *(Note: Sometimes I will add a couple of drops of yellow color at this point).*
5. Add the cake flour a cup or so at the time just until blended.
6. Bake on 325° for about 1 hour 45 minutes.
7. Test for doneness *(toothpick method).*
8. Let cool.

I usually glaze this cake with a lemon glaze, sprinkled with lemon zest

For an added touch, I will sometimes make a lemon whip cream and put dollops on top of the glazed cake. *(Lemon whip cream: 2 cups heavy cream; 1 or 2 drops of yellow color; 2 tablespoons of 10X Confectioner's sugar; ½ teaspoon of lemon extract – whip to desired thickness, but don't let it turn to butter!!!!!!!!!!!!!!!!)*

~ III ~ Fly Away Home

Curried Beef with Sherry

When I make this, I think about my Daddy. He made a wonderful beef stew and this is a variation of his stew. Since I added some wine to this dish, I think he would approve of the variation!

Anytime I'm going to make a beef stew, I buy a large piece of chuck or round and cut the meat into the cubes that I desire. I rarely, if ever, buy what grocers package as stew beef! I find that I can be very economical if I buy a large round or chuck; cut off what I need, and freeze the remainder!

2 pounds stew beef cut in cubes
(Note: Buy a round or chuck roast, and cut the cubes yourself!)

½ cup butter-flavored margarine
¼ cup olive oil
2 cups each – carrot sticks; celery sticks; sliced mini portabellas
10 – 12 small boiler onions
12-14 tiny white or tiny red potatoes
½ cup All-purpose flour, mix into the flour
3 TABLEspoons Curry powder, garlic powder, onion powder
1 TABLEspoon ea. salt, black pepper, dry mustard
½ TABLEspoon ea. cumin, thyme
3 TABLEspoons Worcestershire sauce

Ham Bones memoirs of a southern cook

1 TABLEspoon Soy sauce
½ cup Cream sherry
3 cups water

Instructions:

1. dust the beef in the flour and slowly brown with the margarine and olive oil in a large Dutch oven.
2. Remove when browned, the de-glaze with 1 cup of water.
3. Add back the browned beef, then all the veggies.
4. Add the Worcestershire sauce, sherry and water.
5. Cover and put in oven at 250° for 3 ½ hours.

Chicken in Celery Cream

Fresh celery is abundant year-round. When slowly sautéed it can make a wonderful topping for chicken. I serve this dish on a bed of flavorful turmeric rice.

**You will need a large fry pan;
as well as a 9 x 12 baking dish; foil!**

1 medium fryer chicken – cut up
1 TABLEspoon olive oil
1 TABLEspoon Yard Bird dust
2 stalks celery, minced
1 large white onion, diced
¼ cup All-purpose flour
1 cup whole milk
1 cup water
1 TABLEspoon yellow prepared mustard
1 teaspoon each salt, white pepper, dry mustard

Instructions:

1. Put olive oil in very hot fry pan, and allow oil to get hot as well.
2. Add chicken pieces, skin down – immediately turn down heat and slowly brown the chicken.
3. Remove chicken and arrange in 9 x 12 baking dish.

4. Add the celery and onions to the fry pan and sauté slowly until just tender.
5. Add the all-purpose flour, prepared mustard and water and bring to a low boil. Then add the milk, dry mustard, salt and pepper.
6. Bring to a boil; then pour over the chicken.
7. Cover chicken with foil and bake at 325° for 1 hour.

Broiled Salmon Cakes

**Preheat oven: 350 ° – Butter or spray olive oil
on ½ sheet cookie pan**

2 large or jumbo eggs
½ teaspoon table salt
1 TABLEspoon Dijon-style mustard
1 TABLEspoon Texas Pete hot sauce or Tabasco sauce
1 teaspoon Cayenne pepper
1 teaspoon red pepper flakes
1 TABLEspoon dry parsley flakes
½ teaspoon celery seed
¼ cup chopped onion
¼ cup chopped celery
¼ cup diced red, yellow and green bell pepper
¼ cup mayonnaise
¼ cup Panko (Japanese-style) bead crumbs
1 ½ pounds coarsely-chopped salmon
(do NOT use canned salmon)

Instructions:

1. Use whisk and mix all ingredients in large bowl ***except for bread crumbs and salmon***.
2. Once mixed, slowly stir in bread crumbs and salmon.
3. Use large ice cream scoop and make large generous

salmon balls. Lay on greased cookie sheet and use bottom of glass to flatten slightly so that you have a salmon cake.

4. Broil on 350° for 15 minutes. You should have a nice crispy brown crust and a moist inside to these cakes.

5. Serve with your favorite remoulade sauce.

Beaver Creek Remoulade

1 cup real mayonnaise
½ cup sour cream
½ cup tomato sauce
2 TABLEspoons Dijon mustard
1 TABLEspoon white vinegar
1 TABLEspoon Worcestershire sauce
1 TABLEspoon Texas Pete hot sauce or
1 TABLEspoon Tabasco sauce
1 teaspoon red pepper flakes
1 TABLEspoon dry parsley flakes
1 TABLEspoon Paprika
½ cup chopped onions
2 cloves of fresh garlic finely chopped

Instructions:

1. Put onion and garlic in food processor and chop/grind until rather fine!
2. Next, add all other ingredients to food processor and pulse until all mixed.
3. Pour in plastic bowl, put on cover and chill a few hours before using.

Stuffed Tomatoes

This is a one-dish meal as an entrée for two; or can be an appetizer for 4.

To assure a nice, tender and moist breast, I poach them in a simmering mixture of water, lemon zest and a sprig of Rosemary! The trick to poaching so that you don't get rubbery, tough breasts, is to bring the liquid to a rapid/hard boil; then immediately turn heat down that you only have hot liquid with a low simmering bubble to it. Then place the breast in it; cover and let simmer for 15-20 minutes until done. Remove from water and sit on paper towel to absorb the liquid.

4 large ripe, but firm, beefsteak tomatoes
2 poached, boneless, skinless chicken breast - chopped
8 pitted green or black olives - chopped
1 stalk of celery - diced
½ green bell pepper – diced
½ cup grated Parmesan cheese
1 8-oz brick of cream cheese
½ teaspoon each of parsley, white pepper, cayenne pepper, celery seed
1 cup shredded 3-cheese blend
1 cup crumbled crisp cooked hickory bacon

~ III ~ Fly Away Home

Instructions:

1. Cut off a cap of each tomato. When cutting the tomato, use an angle so that when you remove the cap, it looks like a spinning top. What you should then have of the tomato is a conical cavity in which to put the stuffing!
2. In a bowl whip the cream cheese.
3. Then, add all ingredients and mix until you get a fluffy mixture.
4. Use an ice cream scoop and stuff each tomato.
5. Sprinkle top with shredded 3-cheese blend and crumbled bacon.
6. Bake on 425 for 15 minutes or until tops are golden brown and cheese has melted nicely.

Orange Glazed
Cornish Game Hens

Almost invariably, when I roast Cornish game hens I will glaze them with a spirited orange glaze. I serve these hens with a cranberry-orange-pecan rice medley for an elegant presentation. If serving the one side, then one bird per dinner guest. If serving as luncheon fare, one-half bird per luncheon guest! Recipe for the orange glaze follows this recipe.

Pre-heat oven to 500° - Roast birds at 400°.

4 Cornish game hens
1 TABLEspoon olive oil

Roasting Rub:
2 TABLEspoons salt or salt substitute
plus, 1 TABLEspoon each – black pepper, orange zest, turmeric, celery seed, sweet basil, rosemary, dry mustard

Instructions:

1. Wash birds and dry by sitting on paper towels.
2. Elevate birds on a meat rack; set rack on a cookie pan and refrigerate uncovered overnight.
3. Brush birds with olive oil and liberally sprinkle with the roasting rub.

4. Roast the birds UNcovered for 45 minutes or until skin is crisp, golden brown.
5. Remove birds from oven and let them rest for 10 minutes.
6. Brush on orange glaze (see recipe).
7. Return birds to oven and turn oven off.
8. Close oven door and let birds sit in hot oven for 15 minutes for glaze to set.

Duck:

This recipe also works well for ducks. When preparing the duck for roasting, do not brush with the olive oil. Instead, use a meat fork and puncture the duck several time so that the rendered fat drains well; then, sprinkle the rub liberally. Though the duck will be elevated on a meat rack, use a deep roasting pan, as ducks will render quite a bit of fat. Save your seasoned duck fat—it's delicious in many dishes.

Orange Glaze
(for Cornish Hens)

When I roast Cornish game hens, I glaze them with this spirited glaze that brings out the meat along with the cranberry-orange-pecan rice I use as the side dish!

Bring to a rolling boil:
1 cup water
1 cup orange juice
½ cup light brown sugar
½ cup granulated sugar

At the soft-ball stage,
take off the heat and stir in:
1 TABLEspoon fresh orange zest
½ teaspoon orange extract
½ cup Grand Marnier or Cointreau
¼ cup clover honey

Then, paint the birds with the glaze and return to the warm oven to let them sit for just a few minutes so that the glaze adheres!

Rice Barbados

There is no question in my mind that cuisines from one region to another are related, if none other than by virtue of migration of citizens from one place on the globe to another. This really proved true to me when I traveled to Bridgetown, Barbados and enjoyed two different seafood dinners: Flying fish; and sword fish. On both occasions, the side dish was a medley or lentils and rice. It was no different than what we called Hoppin' John in the states –done with a different pea!

I don't wait to make this dish just when I'm having seafood – I also love it with chicken, beef, pork. To accommodate my taste for a bit of a kick, I also include some spicy additions, as well as some peppers, celery and onion for a bit more flavor! If I'm going to make this a one-dish meal, I simply cook my meat in the pot with the rice ending up with a sort of "Rice Bog" of a dish!

1 small bag of lentil peas
½ cup water
2 slices fat back

Seasoning Mix:
1 teaspoon each - salt, pepper, garlic powder, onion powder plus, 1 TABLEspoon each - red pepper flakes, cayenne pepper

1 TABLEspoon olive oil
1 diced large onion
2 cloves garlic, finely minced
1 each, diced – red, green and yellow bell pepper
½ cup finely diced celery
¼ cup water, also
2 cups water
1 cup uncooked long-grain rice

Instructions:

1. In a hot sauce pot, add the fatback and ½ cup of water and slowly bring to a boil.
2. Pour off the water, then continue to cook on very low heat until fat back is light brown, the skin on it is crisp and there's a TABLEspoon of bacon fat in the pot.
3. Add the lentils peas, onion, garlic, bell peppers and diced celery and sauté on low heat until coated with the bacon fat.
4. Add 2 cups water, bring to a rapid boil – then reduce heat, cover and simmer the lentils for 1 hour. Lentils cook quickly – you will know that they are done as they will double in size as well as be fork tender for tasting a spoonful.
5. You should have about 1 cup of water left in your pot; add another one cup and bring up to temperature.
6. Add 1 cup of long-grain rice and continue to simmer for another 20 minutes or until rice is done and tender. *(Do not overcook the rice. As soon as you see a faint line on the middle of the rice gain,*

completely turn off the heat and pour off any excess water!)

7. Remove from the heat, keep covered and let the steam finish everything up! Just before serving, do a quick fork stir to fluff up the medley.

Cranberry~Orange
Pecan Rice

For some reason, as a youngster I did not care too much for rice – I preferred potatoes. As I matured, I enjoyed rice – especially my Mother's Rice Pilaf or sometimes called Pearlo Rice! It started me to experimenting with rice and coming up with different medley combinations!

This is a sweet-savory rice that I always make when I do Cornish Game Hens with an orange glaze that I have shown elsewhere in this book. Fresh cranberries do not work well for this dish – so, the recipe calls for dried cranberries – what we now commonly refer to as craisins! Butter-roasted toasted pecans add an unbelievable crunch and flavor to this dish. This recipe will serve 8 dinner guests.

2 cups uncooked, long-grain rice
½ cup water
4 cups chicken stock or water

Seasoning Mix:
1 teaspoon each -salt, pepper, garlic powder, onion powder, turmeric plus, 1 TABLEspoon each - red pepper flakes, cayenne pepper, parsley flakes, fresh orange zest

¼ cup frozen orange juice concentrate

~ III ~ Fly Away Home

1 teaspoon orange extract
1 TABLEspoon olive oil
1 large yellow onion, diced
1 each, diced - red, green and yellow bell pepper
½ cup finely diced celery
1 cup dried cranberries
1 cup butter-roasted toasted pecans

Instructions:

1   Put the olive oil in a hot sauce pot; add the onion,
    bell peppers and celery and sauté until tender.
    Remove from pan to a waiting plate and set aside.
2   Add the uncooked rice and sauté in the remaining
    oil for 2 minutes, and then add the water and the
    turmeric. Cook until the rice is done.
3   Add the onion, peppers and celery to the rice. Add
    the cranberries, pecans, orange extract, and
    remainder of the seasoning mix – stir to combine.
4   Sprinkle with the ¼ cup of frozen orange juice
    concentrate. Cover and allow the hot rice to heat
    the entire rice medley.

Duck 'n Grits

(with Cointreau Butter)

This is one of those dishes that you make when you want to take good ol' country food like grits and kick it up a bit! Grits on a silver platter – sort of what my Aunt Lucille would call being a little bit shaditty!

1 medium duck breast
1 TABLEspoon olive oil
1 TABLEspoon Yard Bird dust
1 pound salted butter, room temperature
¼ cup fresh-squeezed orange juice
3 TABLEspoons orange extract
1 TABLEspoon fresh orange zest
1 TABLEspoon dry parsley leaves
1 teaspoon Worcestershire sauce
1 teaspoon cayenne pepper
¼ cup Cointreau orange liqueur
2 cups old-fashion grits
4 cups water or chicken stock

Instructions:

1. Put olive oil in a large hot fry pan.
2. Puncture duck breasts with meat fork several times; then place skin-side down in hot olive oil

and slowly brown. Remove from heat, and slice duck breast in ¼-inch slices on the diagonal bias!

3. Pour off excess duck fat from fry pan. Dust the sliced duck breast and return to fry pan and add the orange juice. Simmer on low heat for 10 minutes.

4. Remove from heat; sprinkle with parsley leaves cayenne pepper and Worcestershire sauce.

5. In small mixing bowl add butter, orange extract, orange zest and beat until fluffy. Pour in liqueur and slowly blend.

6. Transfer compound butter to a plastic bowl and chill until very firm.

7. In a large pot, add 2 cups of grits, plus 1 teaspoon of salt to 4 cups of boiling water or chicken stock. Slowly simmer covered until grits are done. For a stiff grits, remove cover and allow liquid to evaporate until grits are of desired thickness.

8. Pour grits into center of silver meat platter. Make a small indention in the center of the grits. Place the sliced simmered duck in its sauce to the grits. Add two or three scoops of the compound butter.

9. Place remaining Cointreau butter on table for diners to help themselves for additional butter with their individual servings.

Marvin's
Calf Liver Sauté

In the south we love smothered liver and onions. It is especially good with some rice, peas and carrots, a hot buttered biscuit and a glass of ice tea. This is a take on calf liver that my childhood friend Marvin did as an alternative to an onion gravy. The trick to doing liver in this manner is the extremely low temperature and the very slow cooking process. This dish is delicious!

**You will need a large cast-iron fry pan
2 - oblong glass dishes (at least 9 x 12)
Tongs**

1 TABLEspoon olive oil
1 TABLEspoon unsalted butter
2 medium-size slices of liver (I use calf's liver)
½ cup evaporated milk
1 cup Italian-seasoned bread crumbs

Instructions:

1. Pour the evaporated milk in one of the 9 x 12 dishes. Add the 4 slices of calf's liver. Allow to marinate for 30 minutes.
2. Put seasoned bread crumbs in second 9 x 12 dish.
3. Heat cast-iron fry pan until very hot. Add olive oil

~ III ~ Fly Away Home

and immediately turn down the heat to low. Then, add the butter and allow to melt.

4. Dredge liver in seasoned bread crumbs and sauté very slowly on low heat until done.

Red River
Beef Stew

1 - 2 ½ pound beef roast (round; chuck; or sirloin)
3 large Russet white potatoes, peeled and cut into chunks
12 small boiling onions
4 large carrots – peeled and cut into chunks
2 stalks celery, cut into chunks
1 - 8 oz pkg frozen sweet peas
½ cup Roast beef rubbing dust (see recipe in this book)
¼ cup all-purpose flour
¼ cup olive oil
2 cups cold water
¼ cup burgundy wine
2 TABLEspoons sour mash whiskey

Instructions:

1. In a dry sauté plan pour ¼ cup of flour and continuously stir until flour cooks and becomes a medium-dark brown, with a bit of a nutty smell. Then remove from heat.
2. On top of stove with burner on medium high, get a *"dry"* Dutch oven very hot.
3. Pour olive oil in the hot Dutch oven; then get the olive very hot!
4. Immediately turn the stove down to upper low – just below medium.

~ III ~ Fly Away Home

5. Dust the beef and put in Dutch oven; slowly brown all sides *(For later use, save the remaining dust and add to the browned flour from step 1 above).*
6. Add the vegetables to the Dutch oven, stirring to coat all in the hot oil.
7. Add the water and the burgundy wine and sour mash whiskey - cover and simmer for 30 minutes.
8. Combine ½ cup water with the cooked flour and leftover dust to make a slurry. Then, pour into the stew pot.
9. Cover and continue to simmer for 30 minutes – stew should be thickened.
10. Remove from heat and allow sitting for 20 minutes before serving.

Lamb Chops Flambé

A friend came to visit and I wanted to impress her with my cooking skills! I made these chops and she loved them. You can use center-cut or loin-cut chops. When using the center-cut, I "French" the bones to make it even more impressive. I have a trivet at the table so that I can actually light the cognac at the dining table! Dinner guests love the dazzle!

You will need a large sauté pan (preferably 9-inch)

4 thick center-cut lamb chops
1 teaspoon olive oil
1 teaspoon unsalted butter
¼ cup VSOP cognac

Seasoning Mix:
1 teaspoon each of: salt, pepper, tarragon, chopped rosemary, dry mustard

Garnish:
6 TABLEspoons of fresh chopped mint leaves

Instructions:

1. Sprinkle seasoning mix on chops and let rest in refrigerator for 20 minutes.

~ III ~ Fly Away Home

2. Heat sauté pan until very hot; remove from heat.
3. Add olive oil, then butter to melt.
4. Return pan to heat, add seasoned chops and sauté 2 minutes.
5. Turn chops over and sauté for 1 minute, then pour the cognac on the chops and light. Allow the cognac to flavor the chops. When the flame is finished, garnish with the chopped mint leaves.
6. Let chops rest for 2 minutes before serving.

Crème de Menthe
Lamb Roast

I have loved roasted leg of lamb ever since we got it as a rare spring treat during my youth. It was always served with a mint jelly. My appreciation for it was tremendously elevated during a sojourn to Ireland where I had been invited as a special guest to the Judges' Dinner the night before the famous St. Patrick's Day Irish Kennel Club Dog Show at the Royal Dublin Society. The lamb was roasted to perfection and served with a true mint sauce.

This recipe is my interpretation of that wonderful experience. I like a bone-in whole leg of lamb for this roast; so I visit a butcher rather than purchase the pre-packaged lamb roast in the supermarket! I roast this lamb very slowly for best results!

Pre-heat oven to 500° – Roast at 300°

1 medium-size leg of lamb *(bone-in)*
4 TABLEspoons olive oil
2 TABLEspoons unsalted butter melted
4 medium-size white onions *(quartered)*
4 medium-size carrots *(peeled & cut in thirds)*
4 medium-size parsnips *(peeled & cut in thirds)*
3 stalks celery *(washed & cut in thirds)*
8 medium-size white potatoes *(washed, peeled and quartered)*

~ III ~ Fly Away Home

Seasoning Mix:
1 TABLEspoon each – salt, pepper, finely minced rosemary, dry mustard

Mint Sauce:
3 cups water
¼ cup granulated sugar
1 ½ cup fresh mint leaves *(finely chopped)*
¼ cup Crème de menthe liqueur

Instructions:

1. Wash leg of lamb, then dry off with paper towel. Trim exposed "silver" and about ⅓ of the fat. Then rub 2 TABLEspoons of the olive oil on the lamb. Sprinkle half of seasoning mix and let rest in refrigerator for 2 hours; preferably overnight!
2. In large roasting pan, toss prepared vegetables in the remaining 2 TABLEspoons of olive oil, along with the 2 TABLEspoons of melted butter, then sprinkle the remaining seasoning mix on them *(Make sure all the vegetables are well seasoned with the mix!)*.
3. Put meat rack in roasting pan on top of the vegetables. Then, sit the seasoned leg of lamb on the rack.
4. Put lamb in the oven for 15 minutes while it is on 500°. Then, remove the roasting pan, pour 1 cup of water in the roasting pan; cover with large piece of foil, return to oven at cook covered for 1 hour at 300°.

5. Then remove the roasting pan, remove the foil, return to oven and roast UNcovered for 1 hour at 300°.
6. Remove the lamb and let rest for 30 minutes before serving. The vegetables should be placed in a large baking dish to be warmed before serving.
7. To make the mint sauce, bring 3 cups of water and ¼ cup of sugar and the chopped mint leaves to a hard boil. Cook until half the liquid is reduced and syrup begins to thicken. Remove from the heat and let cool down until warm, but not hot! Stir in the Crème de menthe. Serve the mint sauce on the side.

Potato-Onion Au Gratin

(savory cheese custard)

My mother use to make a dish called scallop potatoes, which was sliced white potatoes in custard! When she would add cheese to the dish, she called them potatoes au gratin. Both were delicious. During my travels, I had pearl onions in creamy custard that was also delicious. I've combined them both for a potato-onion medley of sorts. I think you'll find this a nice side dish to accompany a roasted chicken! Just as good with a broiled chop or steak as well. All I add: A few stalks of buttered seasoned asparagus; and a glass of wine!

You will need an 8 x 8 square baking dish

2 medium Russet potatoes
1 medium White onion
2 cups evaporated milk
¼ cup sour cream
¼ stick unsalted butter
3 cups shredded 3-cheese blend
1 teaspoon each – salt, ground black pepper, garlic powder, onion powder
½ teaspoon cayenne pepper

Instructions:

1. Wash and peel potatoes. Peel the onion. Slice both of them very thin.
2. Place the ¼ stick of butter in the baking dish and allow the butter to melt slowly in the oven. Then, remove from oven and set aside.
3. In a medium-size steel bowl whisk together the milk, sour cream and spices.
4. Arrange a layer of sliced potatoes in the buttered dish; then a layer of sliced onion; add a ½ cup of the savory custard atop them. Sprinkle with 1 cup of the shredded cheese blend. Repeat this routine until all the potatoes and onions and custard have been used. Make sure to use the last amount of shredded cheese as the top layer.
5. Bake at 350° for 35 – 45 minutes; longer if at high altitude.

Scalloped Potato~Onion Bake

(savory cream custard – no cheese)

**You will need an 8 x 8
square baking dish**

2 medium Russet potatoes
1 medium White onion
2 cups evaporated milk
¼ cup sour cream
¼ stick unsalted butter
1 teaspoon each salt – ground black pepper, garlic powder, onion powder
½ teaspoon cayenne pepper
¼ cup Panko-type Japanese bread crumbs for topping

Instructions:

1. Wash and peel potatoes. Peel the onion. Slice both of them very thin.
2. Place the ¼ stick of butter in the baking dish and allow the butter to melt slowly in the oven. Then, remove from oven and set aside.
3. In a medium-size steel bowl whisk together the milk, sour cream and spices.

4. Arrange a layer of sliced potatoes in the buttered dish; then a layer of sliced onion; add a ½ cup of the savory custard atop them. Repeat this routine until all the potatoes and onions and custard have been used. Sprinkle the bread crumbs on top.

5. Bake at 350° for 35 – 45 minutes; longer if at high altitude.

Cabbage
(with bacon)

In the south, we love cabbage. I particularly love it with rice on the side and a fried pork chop! But, when I make such a dinner, I make sure to invite over too many people so that there's not enough for me to stuff myself – 'cause if there's more in the pot, I surely will do so!

1 large cabbage, julienne slices like cole slaw
1 thick slice salted pork [streak-o-lean bacon (minced)]
1 teaspoon each - salt, white pepper, black pepper, red pepper flakes
1 TABLEspoon granulated sugar
½ cup water

Instructions:

1. In a large very hot fry pan (I use my cast-iron skillet), add the minced bacon. Cook it very slowly until light brown and crisp. Remove and place on paper towel.
2. In the hot pan add the sliced cabbage, the salt, peppers, sugar and water.
3. Immediately cover, turn down the heat to very low and let cook for 5 minutes.

4. Remove the cover, turn the cabbage and cook another 5 minutes.
5. Remove from heat, cover and allow the remaining steam to finish the cooking.
6. Do not overcook the cabbage until it becomes too soft – you will lose the flavor of it if you do so.

Sweet Peas and Rice

Any kind of peas can be used for this dish. I love sweet peas and so use them when making this to go with my sautéed calf liver

1 pound of fresh shelled sweet peas, or
1 bag of frozen sweet peas – thawed & drained
1 TABLEspoon of melted bacon fat
Seasoning Mix: 1 teaspoon each – salt, pepper, granulated sugar
1 diced shallot or ½ diced small onion
½ finely-diced red bell pepper
½ finely-diced yellow bell pepper
1 teaspoon Worcestershire sauce
2 cups water
1 cup uncooked long-grain rice

Instructions:

1. In a hot sauce pot, add the TABLEspoon of melted bacon fat.
2. Add the diced shallot, diced bell peppers and sauté until just tender.
3. Add the sweet peas, seasoning mix, Worcestershire sauce and cup of water.
4. Bring to a boil, then turn heat down to a slow boil and slow boil for 10 minutes.

5. Reduce heat to a simmer, cover pot and simmer for 20 minutes.

6. Add 1 cup of long-grain rice and continue to simmer for another 20 minutes or until rice is done and tender. *(Do not overcook the rice. As soon as you see a faint line on the middle of the rice gain, completely turn off the heat, cover pot and set aside so that steam can finish the cooking of the rice.)*

Creamy
Summer Soup

This soup can easily be a vegan dish by omitting the ham shank and streak-o-lean bacon; and also substituting soy milk instead of using the evaporated skim milk. I have a serving of this as a one-dish luncheon meal during warm summer months. You really do not need any seasoning in this soup as the potpourri of vegetables provide a wonderful bouquet that's of great taste! This soup can also be served chilled similar to a vichyssoise . When served chilled, you should add a bit of Chablis to it — perhaps ¼ cup!

1 ham shank
3 quarts of water
2 slices streak-o-lean bacon
2 ears of sweet corn on the cob (cut off kernels)
4 stalks of celery (cut in THIN slices)
6 baby portabella (cut in thick slices)
1 large white onion (thick slices)
1 yellow banana squash (slice thick)
1 green zucchini squash (slice thick)
10 pencil asparagus (cut, but careful not to use the end wood)
4 tomatoes (cut in quarters – do NOT remove skin and seeds)
4 medium new red potatoes (cut in cubes)

4 medium carrots (cut in large chunks)
1 red bell pepper (cut in large chunks)
1 green bell pepper (cut in large chunks)
1 cauliflower (cut in large florets)
1 can evaporated skim milk
4 TABLEspoons all-purpose flour

Instructions:

1. In a large stock pot, slowly brown ham shank and streak-o-lean bacon on medium heat.
2. Add 2 quarts of the water to the stock pot with the meat and bring to a rapid boil.
3. Add all the vegetables to the stock pot of boiling water and wait for return of the boil. Once boiling, immediately turn heat down so that you have a simmer. Let this pot of vegetables simmer for about 1 hour. Watch it for evaporation, as you will need to add the 1 quart of water after about an hour.
4. Using a spider, or slotted spoon remove vegetables from stock. Place in food processor or blender; add evaporated milk and flour and puree/liquefy.
5. Return the very thick puree to the stock pot. You should have about a quart of vegetable stock; if not, add enough water to make up a quart.
6. Simmer another 30 minutes and remove to cool down before serving this summer soup.

~ III ~ Fly Away Home

Carolina Bisque

During my first summer in New York City, I was determined to see the entire five boroughs all at once – youthful energy ready to be expended! What I did do all at once was find one of those great restaurants that one hears so much about; and tried something that I had heard of but never experienced – lobster bisque! Being the brash young fella I was at the time, I concluded that it was dressed-up tomato soup with lobster in it! Well my goodness, I thought, this will work fine with crab and shrimp and some of the other seafood we have in our southern waters! When I returned home at the end of the summer, I was quick to tell my mother of my experience and that I would be coming up with our own "bisque" such as it were!!!!

Providing a little guidance as to ingredients, she smiled and was very encouraging of my trying to be creative! I'm hoping that you will also enjoy this take on a classic French soup that I've done a below-the-Mason-Dixon variation!!!!!

2 cups cooked - small popcorn shrimp
2 cups cooked - Charleston blue crab meat
1 cup poached - red snapper, coarsely minced
1 TABLEspoon olive oil
1 stalk celery, diced
1 medium yellow onion, diced
1 large carrot, peeled, sliced and diced
1 cup each tomato puree, diced tomatoes

3 cups chicken stock or fish stock
1 cup water
¼ cup cream sherry
1 cup heavy whipping cream
¼ cup butter
1 teaspoon each - salt, white pepper, tarragon, dry mustard, cayenne pepper, garlic powder, onion powder

Instructions:

1. Put olive oil in very hot Dutch oven or large stock pot, and allow oil to get hot as well. Add the diced celery, carrots and onion. Cook until tender. Once tender, remove from pot, put in blender or food processor and puree until smooth. Return the puree to the pot.
2. Add the tomato puree and the diced tomato, the water and the chicken or fish stock. Simmer for 30 minutes. Add the spices and the butter and continue to simmer for an additional 15 minutes.
3. Remove from the heat, add the shrimp, crab and diced red snapper. Stir to combine, cover and allow steam to warm the seafood.
4. Just before serving, but while still hot – stir in the sherry and heavy whipping cream.
5. Bisque should be creamy, thick and richly elegant with chunks!

~ III ~ Fly Away Home

Corn Bread Dressing

My cornbread dressing starts with my grand folks Homestead Cornbread recipe. The trick to a good dressing is to make sure that it is not dry! This dressing is a country-style savory-corn-sweet type with an abundance of minced vegetables in it! I also use this dressing when making stuffed pork chops. This recipe makes enough dressing to freeze for the next holiday. If you do not want to freeze any, make only half this recipe.

6 cups The Sisters Finch Homestead Cornbread
(I dry it, then crumble it, and leave it sitting out on the kitchen counter overnight)

The Dressing Seasoning:
¾ cup each – chopped/minced onion, celery, tri-color bell peppers, boiled eggs
½ cup dried parsley
2 TABLEspoon each -- salt, ground black pepper, cayenne pepper, sage, thyme, garlic powder, onion powder, turmeric
2 cups mixture of chicken gizzards, livers – cooked and chopped

First Liquid Mix:
1 cup each whole buttermilk; chicken stock; water
4 large eggs

Second Liquid Mix:
2 cups chicken stock
½ cup buttermilk
¼ cup granulated sugar

Instructions:

1. In a large bowl put the dried cornbread pieces with the dressing seasoning ingredients – toss together and let sit for 10 minutes.
2. In medium-size bowl, whisk together the First Liquid Mix – pour over mixed cornbread mixture and let sit for 15 minutes to soak up all the moisture.
3. Pour ½ of Second Liquid Mix and stir into dressing. You should have a thick "batter". If not yet a batter, add more of the Second Liquid Mix until you have a thick "batter".
4. Pour dressing into large 9 x 12 baking dish and bake at 350 until done. Test with a toothpick (You will have dressing mix that you can put in zipper freezer bags to freeze).

Red Pepper
Savory Biscuits

This is a dinner/supper biscuit that's buttered and served with a beef stew, calf liver or roasted chicken as the main entrée. I developed this recipe to satisfy a craving for a savory bread to eat with a heavy meat dish.

Blend all spices with your hands before cutting in the shortening. Then mash the shortening into the flour mixture as you do not want too many chunks of shortening visible in this dough when you roll it out!

4 cups All-purpose flour
3 TABLEspoons baking powder
2 TABLEspoons parsley flakes

1 teaspoon each –
table salt (iodized),
white pepper,
red pepper flakes,
dry minced onion,
granulated garlic,
granulated sugar

⅓ cup bacon fat drippings, *or ⅓ cup vegetable shortening*
¾ cup whole buttermilk

Instructions:

1. Combined all dry ingredients, then add the bacon fat or shortening and mash with your fingers until well blended.
2. Add buttermilk and combine.
3. Roll dough on floured surface and cut into biscuits.
4. Bake at 400° for 20 minutes – tops should be golden brown.

Spicy-Nutty
Baked Acorn Squash

This recipe will serve four as a vegetarian entrée. When sliced in half, it makes a nice side dish for 8.

4 nice-size acorn squash.
¼ cup melted unsalted butter

Seasoning Mix:
¼ cup light brown sugar
1 TABLEspoon white granulated sugar

1 teaspoon each – salt, pepper, ground cloves, cinnamon, allspice, ginger, nutmeg

¼ cup finely chopped walnuts

Instructions:

1. Pre-heat oven at 350-degrees
2. With a bit of the melted butter, grease a 9 x 12 baking dish
3. Wash and remove seeds from the acorn squash. Slice a bit on the bottom so that they will sit flat. Brush tops and inside of squash with the melted butter and put into the baking dish.

4. Add 1 cup water; and sprinkle squash with half the seasoning mix.
5. Cover with foil and bake for 30 minutes.
6. Remove from oven; uncover; sprinkle the remaining seasoning mix.
7. Bake UNcovered for an additional 10 minutes to set seasoning onto the squash. Then _broil_ for 5 minutes to slightly crisp up the seasoning.
8. Remove from broiler and let rest for 5 minutes before serving.

Hambone's
BBQ Rib Rub

Time to fire up the grill and prove to everyone that you are a Grill Master! You will need a very large bowl to mix this rub! That big bowl that's used to make yeast rolls would be perfect. Once you make this rub, you can store it in one of those zipper-type freezer bags!

2 cups each
Dark brown sugar
White granulated sugar

1 cup each
Iodized table salt
Ground black pepper

½ cup each
Granulated garlic
Onion powder
Dry yellow mustard
Crushed red pepper flakes
Cayenne pepper (¾ cup for a bit more spicy)
Hungarian Paprika

Ham Bones — memoirs of a southern cook

¼ cup each
Ground celery seed
Fresh orange zest

4 TABLEspoons each
Fresh lemon zest
Ground cumin
Ground sage

2 TABLEspoons each
Ground basil
Ground bay leaf

Use a restaurant type salt/pepper shaker.
Shake generously on meat and let it sit for 30 minutes
Put the meat on the grill – and remember – low and slow!

Beer Batter
Fried Fish

One of my friends caught a mess of bass one morning; called me and said that I should come over and help him fry them up! For a change of pace, I decided to introduce him to a beer batter for those bass. If you like English-style fried fish and chips, you will like this batter.

This batter works very nicely with cod, grouper, halibut and Pollock, and other firm-flesh white fish that are great for deep frying. This is great for an outdoor fish fry!

In a bowl mix
2 cups All-purpose flour
1 teaspoon each salt, pepper, dry mustard, cayenne pepper
1 16 oz. can your favorite beer or club soda

Instructions:

1. Scale, clean and filet your fish!
2. Or, have your fishmonger at the seafood store dress and filet some fish for you.
3. Prepare the batter by mixing all the ingredients in a bowl.
4. Dip you fish filet in batter.

5. Then drop into pot of hot oil and fry until light golden brown and crisp.
6. Drain on paper towels.
7. With a slotted spoon, scoop up the crispies in the pot and serve with the fish as a garnish.!

~ III ~ Fly Away Home

Stuffed
Pork Chops

I've been making stuffed pork chops for years; but recently created a pineapple glaze for them. I took these to a potluck dinner and my kennel club colleagues loved them. The chops can be stuffed a day ahead and refrigerated, then baked the day of the dinner.

Pre-heat oven to 500° - Bake chops at 350°

8 double-thick pork chops (I like them 1 ½ – 2 inches thick)
1 clove garlic, finely minced
1 TABLEspoon each - salt, pepper, dry mustard, dark brown sugar, cayenne pepper, onion powder
4 cups un-cooked cornbread dressing

Instructions:

1. With a paring knife cut a pocket into each chop.
2. In a small bowl, mix the garlic and seasonings.
3. Fill each chop with ½ cup of uncooked cornbread dressing.
4. Arrange in two 9 x 12 baking dishes
5. Bake for 45 minutes at 350 degrees.
6. Remove chops and let rest for 10 minutes.

7. Pour on ⅓cup of Pineapple Orange Firecracker Glaze (see recipe) on top of each chop. Return chops to oven and continue to bake another 20 minutes until glaze sets on the chops.

Pineapple~Orange
Firecracker Glaze

Bring to a boil:
1 cup water
½ cup pineapple juice
½ cup orange juice
1 cup granulated sugar

Cook and let reduce and test it for soft-ball candy stage.
Cut off and remove from heat.
Pour into a bowl and –

Stir in:
½ cup orange juice
½ cup pineapple juice
1 cup pineapple tidbits
1 cup mandarin orange sections
1 TABLEspoon of fresh orange zest
1 TABLEspoon of hot sauce
1 TABLEspoon yellow mustard
2 TABLEspoons white vinegar
1 TABLEspoon soy sauce
1 TABLEspoon Worcestershire sauce
1 TABLEspoon cayenne pepper
¼ teaspoon turmeric

Fried Pork Chops

**You will need: Large cast-iron fry pan
(preferably 2 inches deep); or large copper sauté pan
(preferable 2-3 inches deep); or a deep fryer**

Zip-Loc freezer bag (gallon size)
Tongs
oblong glass dish (at least 9 x 12)
4 large thick center-cut pork chops

Dry Ingredients:
4 cups plain flour
1 TABLEspoon each of: salt, pepper, garlic powder,
Adobo seasoning; baking soda; turmeric; dry mustard;
dry rubbed sage; thyme; plus 6 TABLEspoons of dried
parsley flakes

Put all this in the zip-loc bag and shake and mix well
After it is mixed well, then pour in out into the oblong
pan and let it sit there

Liquid: the Marinade:
In the NOW EMPTY zip-loc bag, put in the pork chops;
pour in 2 cups of buttermilk and 1 teaspoon of hot sauce;
squeeze the air out of the bag; zip it close and put this in
the refrigerator for at least 30 minutes to marinade

~ III ~ Fly Away Home

Getting ready to fry:

Heat cooking oil to 360-degrees; then turn it down to 325 degrees.

Take pork chops from bag and coat with flour mixture; let sit for a minute or so to adhere to the buttermilk. Fry until brown.

Yard Bird Dust

This is a great seasoning mix for baked turkey wings, turkey legs, and quartered chicken! I sprinkle it liberally and put a bit of water in the roasting pan and get a nice creamy-type gravy!

In a small stainless steel bowl, combine

2 TABLEspoons salt or salt substitute

plus,
1 TABLEspoon each – garlic powder, black pepper, cayenne pepper, lemon zest or orange zest, onion powder, cumin, turmeric, celery seed, sweet basil

1 cup all-purpose flour

Put in a shaker and dust fowl liberally

Cast-iron Roasted
Splayed Yard Bird

One of the most wonderful versions of roast chicken is to do it in a cast-iron skillet with vegetables. One dish, fully-balanced meal that only needs a crust of bread and smooth jazz playing while dining! For the perfect bird, let it chill in the refrigerator overnight to dry the skin! This will result in an exceptionally crisp skin with super-moist chicken that your diners will think you had catered!

Pre-heat oven to 500° - Roast bird at 425°.

1 medium-size chick *(cut out the backbone so that you can splay the bird)*
1 TABLEspoon unsalted butter, melted

season with **Cast-iron Yard Bird Rub** *(see recipe that follows)*

2 TABLEspoons olive
1 clove garlic, finely minced
1 medium-size and quartered each – yellow onion, yellow beet, purple beet, broccoli crown, white turnip, Russet potato, plus 5 spears of asparagus, 1 crowns of broccoli split in half
¼ cup water

Instructions:

1. Wash the bird and dry by sitting on paper towels. Elevate bird on a meat rack; set rack on a cookie pan and refrigerate uncovered overnight.
2. In a 12-inch cast-iron fry pan, add ¼ cup water
3. In a bowl add cut-up vegetables, olive oil and garlic with ½ the Yard Bird Rub
4. Toss seasoned vegetables to coat then place in cast-iron fry pan
5. Brush bird with melted butter and liberally sprinkle Cast-iron Yard Bird Roasting Rub. Then, set bird on top of vegetables.
6. Roast the bird UNcovered for 1 hour – skin should be crisp, golden brown.
7. Remove bird from oven and let rest for 10 minutes.

Au Jus Yard Bird
Roasting Rub

This is a great seasoning mix for baked turkey wings, turkey legs, and quartered chicken! This recipe makes an au jus when water or a white wine is added to the roasting pan!

In a small stainless steel bowl, combine
2 TABLEspoons salt or salt substitute

plus, 1 TABLEspoon each – garlic powder, black pepper cayenne pepper, lemon zest, onion powder, turmeric. dry mustard, chopped rosemary, celery seed, thyme

Put in a shaker and sprinkle fowl liberally

Hot Steppin' John

My Hot Steppin' John is a variation of the original dish called Hoppin John! I use the peas to add to cooked rice with vegetables and sausage as a spicy medley. It's a different take on a traditional dish that one friend ate and ate and made me promise to give her the recipe! When served with a hot square of corn bread, or some hot buttermilk biscuits with butter – it can be a hearty one- dish meal!

1 small bag of tiny field peas
½ cup water
2 slices fat back, *or*
1 smoked neck bone

Seasoning Mix:
1 teaspoon each - salt, pepper, garlic powder, onion powder
plus 1 TABLEspoon each - red pepper flakes, cayenne pepper

1 TABLEspoon olive oil
1 diced large onion
2 cloves garlic, finely minced
1 each, diced – red, green and yellow bell pepper
½ cup finely diced celery
½ cup shredded carrots

~ III ~ Fly Away Home

½ pound smoked hot sausage, sliced thin on the diagonal
¼ cup water
2 cups water, also another
2 cups water
1 cup uncooked long-grain rice

Instructions:

1. In a hot sauce pot, add the fatback and ½ cup of water and slowly bring to a boil.
2. Pour off the water, then continue to cook on very low heat until fat back is light brown, the skin on it is crisp and there's a TABLEspoon of bacon fat in the pot.
3. Add the field peas and sauté on low heat until coated with the bacon fat.
4. Add 2 cups of water, bring to a rapid boil – then reduce heat, cover and simmer the peas for 1 hour until tender.
5. In a separate sauce pot, bring 2 cups of water to a boil. Then, add 1 cup of long-grain rice and continue to simmer for another 20 minutes or until rice is done and tender. *(Do not overcook the rice. As soon as you see a faint line on the middle of the rice gain, comp-letely turn off the heat and pour off any excess water!)*
6. In a large cast-iron fry pan, heat 1 TABLEspoon of olive oil.
7. Add the sliced hot smoke sausage and cook just until browned.
8. Add the diced onion, minced garlic, diced peppers, celery and carrots and continue to cook just until tender.

9. Add ¼ cup water and bring everything to a quick boil.
10. Remove from stove, then stir in the rice and the drained, cooked field peas.
11. Cover and let the steam finish heating everything up!

Braised Beef Marsala

Pre-heat oven 500° - Braise at 225°

1 4 – 5 pound beef roast (round; chuck; shank; or sirloin)
6 medium white potatoes
12 green onions (2 to 3 times larger than pearl-onion size)
4 large carrots – peeled and split
½ cup Mack's roast beef rubbing dust
¼ cup olive oil
1 cup good Marsala wine
1 cup cold water
1 4 oz can tomato sauce
¼ cup all-purpose flour

Instructions:

1. On top of stove with burner on medium high, get a *"dry"* Dutch oven very hot.
2. Pour olive oil in the hot Dutch oven; then get the olive very hot!
3. Immediately turn the stove down to upper low – just below medium.
4. Dust the beef and put in Dutch oven; slowly brown all sides.
5. Add the vegetables to the Dutch oven, stirring to coat all in the hot oil.

6. Add the water and the Marsala, and tomato sauce - cover and put in the hot oven.

7. Immediately turn oven down to 225°, and braise covered for 2 ½ hours.

8. Remove beef and vegetables from braising liquid. Return Dutch oven "uncovered" to the oven. Now is the time to *whisk in the ¼ cup of flour here if you want your broth to be a thick gravy!* Raise temperature to 350° and allow braising liquid to reduce by half.

9. Remove Dutch oven from the oven; return meat and vegetables to Dutch oven, spooning thickened broth over them. Cover and let sit for 20 minutes before slicing and serving the beef.

~ III ~ Fly Away Home

Roast Beef Dust

This makes a wonderful seasoning for roast beef. I also use it when I am going to braise beef chunks or make a stew. When using the flour in this rub, and a bit of "seasoned water" in the roasting pan, your au jus will be a thin gravy of sorts!

In a small stainless steel bowl, combine
2 TABLEspoons salt or salt substitute

plus, 1 TABLEspoon each – all-purpose flour
(use flour only if you want your au jus to be a gravy)
garlic powder, black pepper, cayenne pepper, dry mustard, meat tenderizer, onion powder

Put in a shaker and dust beef liberally

Beef "Seasoning Water" *for the roasting pan:*

Puree in a blender –
1 ½ cups of water
1 TABLEspoon soy sauce
1 TABLEspoon Worcestershire sauce
2 TABLEspoons dark raisins
1 TABLEspoon vinegar

Texas Crunch Cake

This is a very moist buttermilk pound cake variation of Aunt Emma T's All-Butter Pound Cake. A wonderful coconut-pecan-honey crunch topping makes it a real game changer!

Bake at: 325° - 1 hour, 15 minutes – test for doneness!

For the cake:
2 sticks unsalted butter
2 sticks buttermilk margarine
1 teaspoon butter flavor
1 teaspoon almond extract
1 teaspoon pure vanilla extract
¼ teaspoon yellow food color
1 ¼ cups WHOLE buttermilk
4 oz sour cream
6 large eggs
4 cups granulated sugar
4 cups cake flour
¼ teaspoon salt
½ cup granulated sugar

For the crunch:
½ stick unsalted butter
¼ cup honey
½ cup water
1 cup dark brown sugar

~ III ~ Fly Away Home

1 cup finely ground coconut
1 cup medium-coarse chopped pecans

Instructions:

1. Make the crunch first. Combine in a bowl dark brown sugar; ground coconut; ground pecans; ½ stick unsalted butter. Once blended, spread out on foil-lined cookie sheet and bake for 20 minutes. Should come out crisp like a candy. Let cool completely, then use a mallet and crack into tiny pieces. Reserve for use later as the crunch topping.

For the cake:

2. Cream butter, margarine, flavor, extract, color and sugar until fluffy. Then, add eggs and sour cream slowly and whip it up again until fluffy. Then add the flour and baking powder and salt, along with whole butter milk alternately. Batter should be custard-like!
3. Pour into pound-cake tube pan and bake. When done, let cool completely in the tube pan. Then remove and set out on wire rack.
4. Bring honey, water and butter to a boil. Cook until thickened at soft-ball stage. Remove from heat and allow to cool down a bit. Then, using a pastry brush, paint the top of the cake generously. While still sticky and wet, sprinkle on the crunch quite liberally.
5. Allow cake to set in fridge while crunch and honey set. Allow cake to set out at room temperature for 30 minutes before cutting and serving.

Joe Mack's
Fried Chicken!

I use an old vintage Sunbeam deep-fryer from the 50s to cook this chicken. I am so proud of this fried chicken recipe, I think it is THE fried chicken recipe to have, if I must say so myself! I'm still licking my fingers!!!!!

Dry Ingredients:
4 cups plain flour

1 TABLEspoon each – salt, pepper, garlic powder, paprika; Adobo seasoning; lemon pepper or dried lemon peel; oregano; baking soda; turmeric; dry mustard

6 TABLEspoons of dried parsley flakes

Instructions:

1. Put all this in the gallon-size freezer bag; zip close, shake and mix well
2. After it is mixed well, then pour in out into the oblong pan and let it sit there

Liquid: the Marinade:
3. In the NOW EMPTY gallon-size freezer bag, put in

the cut-up chicken; pour in 2 cups of buttermilk and 1 teaspoon of Texas Pete Hot Sauce; squeeze the air out of the bag; zip it close and put this in the refrigerator for at least 2 hours to marinade. (Overnight is even better!)

Getting ready to fry:

4. Pour in cooking oil (I use peanut oil) and heat to 360-degrees; then turn it down to 325 degrees.
5. Take chicken from bag and coat with flour mixture; let sit for a minute or so to adhere to the buttermilk. After a minute or so, coat it with the flour again before putting it in the hot oil!
6. Slowly fry until color is a nice golden brown. You will know when it's ready, the frying bubbles will slow down and the chicken will begin to rise to the top of the oil! Watch it though – don't let it overcook!
7. Follow this method and you will get my Fried Chicken a la Perfection!!!!!!!!

Broiled Bluefish

Going out of Long Boat Key, near Sarasota to fish for blues with my Daddy and two brothers was a favorite family sport in the 1960s. Many years later, I would find myself fishing for blues off the coast of Montauk, Long Island as the recreational activity during a corporate retreat weekend. A colleague was chatting with me on how he would be preparing his catch upon returning to the city. When I returned with my catch, I tried his preparation method as well – it was delicious! The ingredients make this such a special dish as the Italian-style bread crumbs give it a crunch topping that absorbs the delicacy of the butter/lemon juice mix as well as the lemon zest that kicks it up to a zing-level!!

This recipe serves two people if each is to have a whole fish; or 4 people if the fish is prepared as four filets!

1 9 x 12 sheet-cake pan (or something similar)
2 medium-size bluefish, butterfly dressed
½ teaspoon salt
½ teaspoon granulated garlic
½ teaspoon black pepper
½ teaspoon fresh lemon zest
¼ cup Italian-style bread crumbs

combine 1 TABLEspoon each – olive oil, melted unsalted butter, lemon juice
¼ cup water

~ III ~ Fly Away Home

Instructions:

1. In a 9 x 12 sheet cake pan (or something similar) lay fish skin-side down. Pour the water in the pan – try NOT to pour it on the fish.
2. With flesh-side up, paint the fish with the olive oil/butter/lemon juice mixture.
3. In a bowl, stir and mix the bread crumbs with all the seasonings (including the lemon zest). Sprinkle the mixture on top the painted fish.
4. Broil this for 12 minutes on 400 degrees.

Broiled Flounder

Flounder is one of those fish that it's good just about any way you cook it! Though I love it fried, I often do it in the oven under the broiler with a little enhancement! The walnuts, lemon and cayenne set this off!

1 9 x 12 sheet-cake pan (or something similar)

2 medium-size whole flounder
½ teaspoon salt
½ teaspoon black pepper
½ teaspoon fresh lemon zest
¼ cup – coarsely chopped walnuts
1 teaspoon – ground cayenne pepper per fish
1 TABLEspoon melted butter
¼ cup water

Instructions:

1. In a 9 x 12 sheet cake pan (or something similar) lay fish white-side down. Pour the water in the pan – try NOT to pour it on top of the fish
2. With a pastry brush, paint the fish with the melted butter.
3. In a bowl, stir and mix salt, pepper and lemon zest. Sprinkle the mixture on top the painted fish.

~ III ~ Fly Away Home

4. Broil this for 12 minutes on 400 degrees.
5. Slide fish out of broiler, sprinkle on the walnuts and 1 teaspoon of ground cayenne pepper per fish.
6. Return to broiler and broil an additional 1 minute, 30 seconds!

Hunters' Pie

This is a recipe I created as a tribute to a friend who loves to hunt with his sons. When I got a new freezer for the house, they surprised me and filled it with some of their venison bounty as a Christmas gift. This is sort of a southern take on the traditional shepherd's pie! It's great comfort food that's also a one-dish meal!

2 pounds ground venison; or venison stew meat cut in small cubes
½ cup butter-flavored margarine
¼ cup olive oil

½ cup each – diced carrots; diced celery; chopped mushrooms, diced onions, diced tomato; frozen English peas

16-20 tiny white or tiny red potatoes *(boil in salted water, then mash with ½ cup beef broth; and ½ cup of heavy cream.)*
¼ cup All-purpose flour, *and mix into the flour*
1 TABLEspoon each – garlic powder, onion powder
½ teaspoon salt, black pepper, dry mustard, thyme
3 TABLEspoons Worcestershire sauce
½ cup Bourbon or Jim Beam Whiskey
2 cups water

~ III ~ Fly Away Home

Instructions:

1   Brown the venison in the margarine and olive oil, then remove to an awaiting plate.
2   Simmer the veggies until translucent.
3   In a bowl add the flour mixture and the water – make a slurry and pour in with the veggies. Continue to simmer until you have a nice gravy.
4   Add back the browned venison, stir and mix – you should have a bit of a stew.
5   Add the Worcestershire sauce and whiskey – stir in to blend.
6   Pour this into a 9 x 13 casserole dish.
7   Cover with the mashed potato and bake until golden brown (about 35 minutes on 350°).
8   Let sit and cool down for about 20 minutes – then spoon out and serve.

Chicken Pot Pie

As a young teenager, frozen chicken pot pie was the comfort food for a middle-of-the-night hunger calling when listening to some jazz! When I started cooking from scratch, I tried over and over again to come up with a homemade scratch recipe that would satisfy me. I think you'll like this one, as it is filling, old-fashioned, and has a wonderful flaky crust!

Step 1
In large stock pot with about 3 quarts of boiling water, add:
    1 small whole fryer chicken
    2 stalks celery
    1 large onion (WHITE only)
    2 large carrots (cut into thirds)
    3 teaspoons each salt, pepper, thyme, sage
    3 bay leaves

Immediately, turn down heat and allow bird and veggies to fully cook on a slow boil, and medium-high simmer! *Do NOT cook too fast, or your bird will be tough!*

Once the bird is done, remove to a platter and let it cool down! Once cool, pull the meat off the bone, discard the skin, and cut into large chunks or cubes!

~ III ~ Fly Away Home

Pour all the remaining liquid into a large measuring cup –
you will need it shortly!

Step 2
Then, in the same large stock pot, on very low heat:
    1 stick slowly-melted unsalted butter
    1 ½ cups all-purpose flour

Once the butter and flour are combined that you have the
base for the buerre blanc, add:
    1 ½ cups evaporated milk
    2 cups broth (add water if you do not have enough

Cook slowly until thickened. Set aside to cool down a bit!

Step 3
Stir in to blend:
    3 TABLEspoons granulated sugar
    1 TABLEspoon each – salt, pepper, garlic powder,
    onion powder, thyme, sage, dry mustard, turmeric,
    paprika, dry parsley flakes

Step 4
Once cooled, FOLD in:
    All of the cooked cut-up chicken
    1 ½ cups frozen mixed vegetables
    1 ½ cups frozen pearl onions
    1 cup fresh celery stalk (diced or sliced)

*Consistency should be that of crepe batter. If thicker, add some
water as it will thicken more as the pie bakes! ! ! ! You do NOT
want a dry pie in the end ! ! !*

Step 5
Pour contents into casserole dish. Top with my perfect crust recipe!

Bake on 425° until crust is golden brown!

Coconut-Pecan Pound Cake

This is an extraordinary pound cake that is dense in texture with a wonderful coconut – pecan bottom. This cake presents a fine, moist crumb of great flavor! This cake has been very popular when I use it for potluck gatherings!

Bake at: 325° - 1 hour, 30 minutes – test for doneness!

For the cake:
2 sticks unsalted butter
1 stick buttermilk margarine
1 teaspoon pure vanilla extract
1 ½ teaspoon coconut flavor
1 ¼ cups WHOLE buttermilk
4 oz sour cream
5 large eggs
3 ½ cups granulated sugar
4 cups cake flour
1 TABLEspoon plus 1 teaspoon baking powder
¼ teaspoon salt

For the coconut-pecan bottom:
½ stick unsalted butter
½ teaspoon coconut flavor
½ teaspoon vanilla extract

½ cup all-purpose flour
½ cup 10X confectioner's sugar
1 cup finely-ground coconut
1 cup medium-coarse chopped pecans

Instructions:

1. Make the bottom first. Combine in a food processor: 1 cup flake coconut; ½ cup all-purpose flour; ½ stick unsalted butter. Pulse until texture of lumpy cornmeal! Add pecans, pulse until coarse chopped. Pour out into a bowl and toss with fingers to create a lumpy crumb! Pour loosely into greased/floured pound cake pan.
2. Cream butter, margarine, flavor, extract, and sugar until fluffy. Then, add eggs and sour cream slowly and whip it up again until fluffy. Then add the flour and baking powder and salt, along with whole butter milk alternately. Batter should be custard-like!
3. Pour into pound-cake tube pan and bake. When done, let cool completely in the tube pan. Then remove and set out on cake plate. Bottom will have a coconut-pecan crust to it.
4. Cake should be set in a cake dome or covered cake plate and kept at room temperature.
5. This cake presents a fine, elegant, moist, rich crumb of wonderful flavor! Enjoy!

Buttermilk Crunch Pie

This is a variation of my Grandmother and Aunt Lucille's Buttermilk Pie that they would make from sour milk in the refrigerator. I use whole buttermilk; and when done add a crunchy coconut-pecan topping!

In a blender – for the filling:

3 eggs
1 ¼ cup sugar
1 teaspoon vanilla extract
4 cups whole buttermilk
¼ cup (half of a stick) of melted "salted" butter
1 teaspoon nutmeg
¼ cup bourbon

Instructions:

1. Blend; pour in pie crust *(see recipe elsewhere in this book)* and bake.

I bake at 325 until done. When it stops the wiggle, you know it's done!!!!!

I use a deep dish quiche pie pan! Comes out with lovely

fluted crust that is very flaky with nice presentation for the table!

2. While the pie is baking – chop semi-fine ½ cup of pecans; ½ cup coconut; and stir in 1 cup of light brown sugar, ½ cup of uncooked old-fashion oatmeal. *(Do not use quick or instant oatmeal!)*
3. When pie is done – sprinkle top with ground pecans, coconut and oatmeal and brown sugar mixture.
4. Put back in oven for a few minutes to crisp up a tad! *(Just a soft crisping – **NOT** too hard like a crème brûlée!)*

Medallions of
Venison Flambé

Venison is very lean. This recipe enhances the flavor of the meat with bacon wrapped around the macerated medallions!

Large sauté pan (preferably 9-inch)

4 thick medallions of venison from the tenderloin
4 thick slices hickory-smoked bacon
1 teaspoon olive oil
1 teaspoon unsalted butter

Marinade:
1 TABLEspoon each – salt, pepper, chopped rosemary, dry mustard, finely chopped garlic, finely chopped white onion - mixed in 1 cup of good single-malt Scotch whiskey

Garnish:
1 cup mix of chopped pecans, raisins and chopped dried apricots

Instructions:

1. Pour marinade in zippered freezer bag, add medallions and refrigerate for 2-3 hours *(preferably overnight)*.
2. Remove medallions from marinade and wrap each with a thick slice of hickory-smoked bacon.
3. Heat a copper sauté pan until very hot; remove from heat.
4. Add olive oil, then butter to melt.
5. Return pan to heat, add marinated medallions and sauté 2 minutes.
6. Turn medallions over and sauté for 1 minute, then pour the marinade on the chops and tilt the pan to light. Allow the whiskey to flavor the medallions. When the flame is finished, garnish with the chopped pecans, raisins and apricots.
7. Let medallions rest for 2 minutes before serving.

Soft-shell Crabs

The season to get soft-shell crabs is very short; so taking advantage of the time period with this recipe is quite a treat. I only serve a few spears of steamed asparagus and carrot sticks with this dish, along with a crust of French baguette.

4 medium soft-shell crabs
¼ cup unsalted butter
1 TABLEspoon olive oil
2 teaspoons finely minced fresh garlic
1 TABLEspoon finely minced fresh yellow onion
1 teaspoon each salt, pepper
2 TABLEspoons All-purpose flour
3 TABLEspoons Sauterne or Chablis wine

Instructions:

1. Heat a sauté pan until hot; then add 1 TABLEspoon of olive oil; ¼ cup of butter. Then, turn down heat and allow butter to melt slowly on medium heat.
2. Add the minced garlic and onions and sauté slowly on the medium heat until soft. (Do not let the garlic brown.)
3. Salt and pepper the crabs, then sprinkle them with the flour.

4. Sauté the crabs until lightly browned.
5. Remove from heat, add the white wine and allow to steep covered for 5 minutes before serving.

Shrimp au Vin Buerre

The season of summer is playtime for me when it comes to seafood in the shell. I love it when I have a great bottle of wine at hand that I will use as my major seasoning component.

Shrimp is a great ingredient for sautéing in butter and wine. This recipe is light; is wonderful with noodles tossed in olive oil and minced parsley or over a bed of seasoned rice. An accompaniment of steamed broccoli is just the perfect addition to the plate. This recipe will serve 4 for lunch or 2 for dinner.

16-20 medium shrimp
¼ cup unsalted butter
2 TABLEspoons olive oil
3 cloves finely minced fresh garlic
2 TABLEspoons finely minced fresh yellow onion
1 teaspoon each - salt, pepper
2 TABLEspoons Old Bay seafood seasoning
3 TABLEspoons Sauterne or Chablis wine

Instructions:

1. Heat a sauté pan until hot; then add the 2 TABLEspoons of olive oil; ¼ cup of butter. Then, turn down heat and allow butter to melt slowly on medium heat.
2. Add the minced garlic and onions and sauté slowly

on the medium heat until soft. (Do not let the garlic brown.)

3. Salt and pepper the shrimp, then sprinkle on the 2 TABLEspoons of Old Bay.

4. Sauté the shrimp until coloring of tails begin to turn pink. (This would be about 2 minutes on medium heat.) Turn the shrimp and sauté for 1 additional minute.

5. Remove from heat, add the white wine and allow to steep covered for 5 minutes before serving.

Carolina Steam Pot

Nothing says summer like fresh seafood eaten alfresco! The steam pot is a wonderful way to prepare it. This recipe is a steamed surf and turn that will make sure you've had a great filling when finished. I love to do this as individual steam pots when I use it for the host entrée to serve at kennel club meetings. Individual disposable aluminum round 8-inch pans covered with aluminum foil and punctured with a fork is the perfect steam pot! This recipe will serve 4 hungry diners!

8 large Tiger prawn shrimp *(leave heads & tails intact)*
8 large chunks/nuggets farm-raised catfish
4 medium lobster tails
4 pieces sausage (cut in 4-inch lengths)
4 half-size ears of sweet yellow corn on the cob
8 small pre-cooked half-done red potatoes
4 stalks celery, cut into 8 pieces
4 carrots peeled and cut into 8 pieces
8 cloves fresh garlic
4 small yellow onions
8 teaspoons each - salt, pepper
4 TABLEspoons Old Bay seafood seasoning
2 cans your favorite beer

Instructions:

1. Pre-heat your oven to 500°; once hot, turn oven down to 350°.
2. In four disposable 8-inch round aluminum pans, divide the shrimp, catfish, lobster tails, sausage, corn, potatoes, celery stalks, carrots, garlic and onions equally.
3. In a small bowl mix the salt, pepper and Old Bay seasoning then sprinkle equally among all the pans.
4. Add ¼ can of beer to each pan; then cover each pan with aluminum foil and puncture with a four-prong fork for venting the steam.
5. Put covered pans in 350° and allow to steam for 20 minutes.
6. Remove from oven and sit each pan on a dinner plate and remove the foil covering to serve your diners.

Corn-Sausage Casserole

This is a very substantial one-dish meal that I created starting out with my mother's corn soufflé. I removed the sugar, added some savory spices to make it an entrée. During cool fall evenings, I have this as a comfort-food dinner in an easy chair by the fireplace. A cup of hot tea is all I need to have with it.

Cut kernels of 6 ears of fresh corn, or
1 bag of frozen organic corn - thawed *(also, drain if necessary)*

1 lb, cut into chunks smoked beef sausage, or Kielbasa or country sausage
½ stick (¼ cup) unsalted butter, plus another
½ stick (¼ cup) unsalted butter
2 TABLEspoons All-purpose flour, plus another
2 TABLEspoons All-purpose flour
1 stalk celery, diced
1 medium yellow onion, minced
1 each, diced green, yellow, red bell pepper
5 sliced button mushrooms
1 cup whole milk
1 cup evaporated can milk
1 teaspoon each - salt, white pepper, sage, thyme
½ teaspoon each - dry yellow mustard, cayenne pepper
2 eggs

Instructions:

1. Grease a 9 x 13 oven-safe baking dish with ½ stick of butter.
2. Sprinkle 2 TABLEspoons of All-purpose flour and coat the smeared butter in the dish.
3. In a large bowl combine corn kernels, sausage, celery, onion, peppers, and mushrooms with seasonings – pour into baking dish and set aside.
4. In a blender, combine – 2 TABLEspoons all-purpose flour, whole milk, evaporated milk and eggs – then pour over the corn, sausage and vegetables.
5. Sit baking dish in a larger baking dish (I use my roasting pan).
6. Pour hot water in the roasting pan such that it comes half way up the baking dish.
7. Bake at 350° for 1 hour or until done. Custard should be light brown around the edges.

~ III ~ Fly Away Home

Broiled
Peaches deLeon

This is a great dessert for fellas cooking a meal to impress the lady of the house! It can be made on the BBQ grill; or it can be done inside under the broiler!

Pre-heat oven at 500°
Once the oven reaches temperature, turn on broiler to 350° (low broil)
Have on the ready: 9 x 13 buttered baking pan

2 large freestone peaches
4 TABLEspoons butter
4 TABLEspoons coarsely ground/chopped pecans
4 TABLEspoons brown sugar
2 teaspoons cinnamon
2 teaspoons ginger
2 teaspoons cloves
2 teaspoons nutmeg
2 teaspoons salt
2 teaspoons coarse-ground black pepper
2 teaspoons vanilla
4 TABLEspoon good-quality Bourbon whiskey
1 cup heavy whipping cream
2 TABLEspoons good-quality Bourbon whiskey
1 TABLEspoon superfine granulated sugar

Instructions:

1. With a paring knife, cut peaches in half; remove pits; arrange in 9 x 13 baking pan skin-side down.

Melt the 4 tablespoons of butter, then on each of the 4 peach halves,
2. Brush the butter onto upside flesh of peaches.
3. In a bowl, mix the salt, nutmeg, cloves, ginger, cinnamon and brown sugar.
4. Evenly divide and spoon on the spiced sugar mixture over each peach
5. Spoon on 1 TABLEspoon of ground/chopped pecans
6. Spoon on 1 TABLEspoon of good-quality Bourbon whiskey + ½ teaspoon vanilla
7. Broil for 10 minutes. You should see some brown toasting on top of peaches and a bit of bubbling of the brown sugar!
8. Top each peach with a nice liberal dollop of Bourbon Cream deLeon.

~ III ~ Fly Away Home

Peaches Vera

In South Carolina, we grow the very best peaches – they are large and very sweet. My friend Vera knows how much I love peaches, so each year she gives me jars of canned peaches from her weekends of canning activity with her Mom.

This is a great dessert of a spiced peach. I do use fresh peaches for this dish. This is a great dish when served with a couple of butter shortbread cookies, and a glass of Sauterne or Riesling...

2 large freestone peaches
3 cups of water
2 TABLEspoons brown sugar
2 TABLEspoons granulated sugar
2 teaspoons cinnamon
2 teaspoons ginger
2 teaspoons cloves
2 teaspoons nutmeg
2 TABLEspoons apple cider vinegar
2 teaspoons coarse-ground black pepper
2 teaspoons vanilla

Instructions:

1. This dessert is best when the peaches are peeled, and poached whole. However, an alternative

preparation will be to cut peaches in half and remove the pits.

In a large sauce pot, combine
2. Water, sugars, spices, and vanilla
3. Bring to a rapid hard boil
4. Immediately turn heat down to a poaching simmer
5. Place the peaches in the simmering liquid and cover
6. Simmer for 40 minutes until peaches are soft, but NOT mushy!*(They should be a firm soft – like al dente pasta!!!)*
7. Remove peaches from liquid and place in a covered container and completely chill.
8. Pour poaching liquid into separate container (perhaps a glass jar with lid) and completely chill.
9. To serve – Put one peach per diner in a sherbet dish with a bit of the poaching syrup for garnish. On the side, also provide two shortbread cookies.

~ III ~ Fly Away Home

Fabulous
Apple Pie

This is an apple pie that I love to make. I use a variety of apples, give it a hint of lemon, vanilla and rum or brandy flavoring. Put a scoop of Rum Raisin Swirl Ice Cream on a warm wedge of this pie and I think you'll love it as well!

You will need 2 pie crust.
See recipe for perfectly flaky pie crust.

2 apples each – Rome, Braeburn, Winesap, Granny Smith
1 apple Red Delicious
1 fresh lemon
1 ½ cups granulated sugar
3 TABLEspoons corn starch
1 TABLEspoon each - cinnamon, nutmeg
1 teaspoon each - cloves, ground ginger, fresh lemon zest
2 TABLEspoons melted unsalted butter
1 teaspoon Mexican Vanilla extract
1 teaspoon Rum flavoring

Instructions:

1. Peel and slice the apples and put in a large bowl. Squeeze the juice of 1 fresh lemon over them and set aside.
2. In a second bowl, combine all remaining ingredients, then pour over the apples. Gently stir well to make sure that all apples are coated.
3. In a 9-inch pie plate, place your bottom crust. Fill the crust with the apple mixture.
4. Place the second crust on top. Crimp edges; and using a paring knife, cut a few slits in the top crust. With a small melon peeler or teaspoon, puncture a small hole in the middle of the top crust for venting.
5. Bake at 400° for 45 minutes to an hour. Crust should be golden brown.

Tip: Use your paring knife, test the apples by inserting the knife in the venting hole. Apples should be tender, but not mushy!

Blueberry Cream Pie

This is a pie that takes me back to my college days. Blueberries were plentiful during the summer months, and using them to make this open-faced one-crust pie with a whipped cream topping was just the cold slice of pie you'd want to cool your taste buds!

You will need to blind bake 1 dessert pie crust.
See recipe for perfectly flaky pie crust.

4 pints fresh blueberries
2 cups water, plus
1 cup granulated sugar
1 teaspoon each - cinnamon, nutmeg
½ teaspoon fresh lemon zest
¼ cup water
¼ cup corn starch
1 teaspoon vanilla extract
1 pint heavy whipping cream
½ teaspoon vanilla extract
1 TABLEspoon 10X Confectioners' sugar

Instructions:

1.   In a large sauce pot bring 2 cups of water and berries to a hard-rapid boil, then immediately turn

down heat to a simmer. Add the sugar, cinnamon, nutmeg, lemon zest and continue to simmer 20 minutes until berries are softened and liquid is reduced by half.

2. In a second bowl, mix ¼ cup water, cornstarch and vanilla extract into a slurry. Pour into hot blueberry compote and simmer until cornstarch is cooked and mixture is thickened to consistency of custard. Then pour into a medium-size stainless steel bowl, cover with sheet of plastic wrap being sure to touch compote so you don't have a skin on the berry custard. Chill completely.

3. In a small mixing bowl, combine whipping cream, vanilla and 10X sugar. Whip until medium-stiff. Should have a spreading consistency of mayonnaise!

4. Pour the chilled blueberry compote into the baked pie shell.

5. Top with the whipped cream and seal all edges. Return to refrigerator until ready to serve.

6. In a 9-inch pie plate, place your bottom crust. Fill the crust with the apple mixture.

7. Place the second crust on top. Crimp edges; and using a paring knife, cut a few slits in the top crust. With a small melon peeler or teaspoon, puncture a small hole in the middle of the top crust for venting.

8. Bake at 400° for 45 minutes to an hour. Crust should be golden brown.

Tip: Use your paring knife, test the apples by inserting the knife in the venting hole. Apples should be tender, but not mushy!

Fireplace
Pear Crisp

This is an crisp for those cool autumn nights by the fireplace. Use a firm variety of pear such as Bartlett. The crumble for the crisp has the added luxury of nuts to make it a real winner of a quick dessert!

You will need a 9 x 12 buttered oven-proof dish.

8 Bartlett pears peeled, sliced and cut into spoonful chunks

Spice Mixture:
1 cups granulated sugar
¼ cup light brown sugar
3 TABLEspoons corn starch
1 TABLEspoon nutmeg
1 teaspoon each cinnamon, ground ginger, fresh lemon zest
2 TABLEspoons melted unsalted butter
1 teaspoon vanilla extract

Crumble Mixture:
2 cups old-fashion oatmeal
¼ cup light brown sugar

½ cup granulated sugar
1 cup chopped pecans or walnuts
½ cup very cold unsalted butter, cubed

Instructions:

1. Place pears in a large mixing bowl. Add the spice mixture and gently stir to coat all the pears. Pour pears into 9 x 12 buttered oven-proof dish.
2. In a second bowl, combine all crumble mixture an cut the butter into the mixture that you have a clumpy consistency! Pour crumble mixture over top of pears.
3. Bake at 400° for 45 minutes to an hour. Crumble should be golden brown.

Tip: Use your paring knife, test the pears by inserting the knife in a pear in the center of the crisp. Pears should be tender, but not mushy!

Rum Custard
Raisin Ice Cream

**(Note: I use an old-fashion electric pine bucket model
ice cream machine.)**

1. **Slowly bring to a simmering boil**
   1 ½ cups heavy cream
   2 cups half & half milk
   4 cups whole milk

Once hot,

2. **add and dissolve**
   2 cups granulated white sugar
   2 TABLEspoons of rum flavor

3. Stir until all is smooth –set aside and let cool down a bit
   – then, pour contents into bowl of ice cream maker;
   churn according to instructions. When semi-soft ice
   cream forms,

then,

4. Pour in the Rum "custard" to get a swirl/ripple
   throughout the ice cream!
5. Pour or paddle the finished ice cream into disposable
   plastic square dishes with the lid. (This is what I use to

freeze my ice cream. I use the ½-gallon size square dishes with the blue plastic top.)

Rum Custard:
Bring to a boil, then turn down and simmer until thick.

2 ½ cups dark raisins * 1 cup water * ½ cup light brown sugar ½ cup good dark rum

Pineapple-Coconut
Brûlée Quiche

I've always loved coconut custard pie whether the custard was French-style baked or British-style stove top! One of my friends from high school had a group of us over for lunch one day to have some of his Mom's coconut custard pie. With the addition of pineapple tidbits, the pie took on an entirely different personality! One that I loved, I might add! I've changed a couple of things like made it deep-dish in a quiche pan; and added a sugar topping that's caramelized with a torch to give it some additional pizzazzzzzz!!!!!

You will need 1 dessert pie crust.
See recipe for perfectly flaky pie crust.

3 cups grated fresh coconut
2 cups pineapple tidbits (drained)
2 cups half & half milk
½ cup whole milk
1 cup granulated sugar
2 large eggs
1 teaspoon coconut flavor
½ teaspoon vanilla extract
½ cup light brown sugar
½ cup white granulated sugar
½ cup medium-ground pecans or walnuts (your choice)

Instructions:

1. Press the pie crust into an 8-inch quiche pan. Pre-bake the crust at 400° for 20 minutes. Then remove from oven and let cool for another 20 minutes.
2. In a blender, combine all ingredients *except* the pineapple tidbits.
3. Place all of the pineapple tidbits into the dessert crust. Then, pour the blended custard into the crust as well.
4. Bake at 325° for 45 minutes until done. As this is custard, and ovens differ, test to assure cooking is complete. Once done, remove from oven and let cook down to room temperature. Once cooled, place the quiche in the refrigerator and chill for at least 4 hours or until very cold! *(Tip: Use your paring knife, test that the custard is done by inserting the knife in the middle of the pie. When removed, knife should be clean!)*

For the sugar-crunch topping:

5. In a small bowl, combine the ½ light brown sugar, ½ cup white sugar and ½ cup ground nuts. Once mixed, pour over the chilled quiche. Do NOT press down – the topping should be rather loose on top.
6. With a kitchen torch, caramelize the topping until the sugar is browned. (Do not over-torch as the sugar will burn!) If you do not have a kitchen torch, you can put the sugar-crunch-topped quiche under your broiler, but watch it every 1 minute to monitor and make sure that the sugar does not burn.

~ III ~ Fly Away Home

Broiled
Catfish Piccata

Living in landlocked Dallas has its definite drawbacks – seafood is priced at a premium here! Catfish, on the other hand, is relatively cheap. And, of course as stated in the description to my Daddy's Catfish Stew, I generally hated catfish as a youngster! But, I am such a fish/seafood lover, I had to figure out a way to have fish at an affordable price! I love Veal Piccata and Chicken Piccata, so decided to experiment with doing a piccata preparation using fish! And, here you have it – Broiled Catfish Piccata! This dish is tremendously inexpensive – the cost of the whole meal was less than $4.00 (catfish, carrots and asparagus)! The Carrots and Asparagus in Parsley Butter recipe follow this recipe.

I was spoiled by NYC with its Bluefish from Montauk! This recipe is very similar to the way I use to cook my bluefish; and it will do well with any firm-flesh seafood, so please vary your choices (Bluefish, salmon, Boston Scrod, cod, grouper, black sea bass, snapper)!

For each dinner guest for whom you are preparing, you will need:

1 large filet of fresh catfish
½ teaspoon of olive oil
4 tablespoons water
1 tablespoon butter

1/6 of a large lemon (a wedge), which will provide
1 tablespoon lemon juice
6 cloves of fresh garlic
1 tablespoon of Italian-seasoned bread crumbs
½ teaspoon salt, pepper, smoked paprika, onion powder, garlic powder, cumin
1 tablespoon Panko (Japanese-style) bread crumbs

Instructions:

1. Preheat oven to 500° so that oven is very hot.
2. In a cold, medium-size cast-iron skillet, add the water.
3. Lay the filet of fish in the skillet, flat side down.
4. Spray ½ teaspoon of olive oil on top of the fish.
5. Put 1 tablespoon of unsalted butter in the middle of the top the fish.
6. In a small bowl mix the Italian-seasoned bread crumbs, salt, pepper, paprika, onion powder, garlic powder and cumin. Stir to mix. Sprinkle on top of filet of catfish.
7. Squeeze the juice of the lemon wedge on top of the breaded fish.
8. Sprinkle the Panko (Japanese-style) bread crumbs on top of the breaded fish.
9. Using a serrated knife, cut the used lemon wedge in strips and add to the pan.
10. Add 6 fresh garlic cloves to the pan.
11. Turn oven down to 350°, switch to "broiler" setting.
12. Place fish under broiler for 15 minutes or until done.

Carrots & Asparagus
(with Parsley–Butter Sauce)

For each dinner guest for whom you are preparing, you will need:

1 large, or 2 medium fresh carrot
5 large, or 8 pencil fresh asparagus
2 TABLEspoons dried parsley flakes
1 ½ cups water
1 TABLEspoon butter
½ teaspoon salt, pepper

Instructions:

The trick to this dish is to <u>not</u> overcook the asparagus! A minute too long of cooking and they will go limp! When I make this dish, I turn off the heat and let the steam cook the carrots!

Note: The 1 ½ cups of water assumes you are preparing for one dinner guest. If you have more carrots to cook, you want <u>enough water to only just cover the carrots</u>!

1. Peel and slice on the diagonal, the carrots.
2. In a sauté pan, add the carrots and water – bring to a boil.
3. Turn heat down and simmer for 10 minutes.
4. TURN OFF the heat at this point!

5. Drain off water leaving only ¼ cup in the pan.
6. Add the asparagus, parsley, butter, salt and pepper.
7. Cover the pan with heavy-duty aluminum foil and let the steam cook the asparagus.
8. Just before serving, the butter would have melted into a seasoned butter sauce. Stir the carrots and asparagus gently in the butter sauce before transferring to a serving dish.

~ III ~ Fly Away Home

Lemon-Pepper
Braised Chicken
(oven-stewed chicken)

For as long as I can remember, my mother, all her sisters, my grandmother and all her sisters use to catch every sale on roasting hens at the local Piggly Wiggly, Winn-Dixie or A&P. Though most times they would roast these hens, many times they would "stew" them because they were tough birds! I particularly loved the stewed chicken my mother would make because she would add celery, onion and carrot to the pot, cover it and just let it simmer away! Her secret seasoning that gave this chicken its superb flavor was ground thyme!

This recipe is homage to all the women in my family famous for catching the sale on hens at the local food store! I enhanced the flavor a bit by adding lemon pepper, which really wakes up the chicken. I cook this with breast intact with skin and rib bones. Of course, traditionally you would use a whole cut-up chicken or hen and all parts are stewed! I do not use boneless-skinless breast for this recipe! (Just a quick note – I do not buy commercial lemon-pepper seasoning. I do not like additives in my food, and it's too easy to make lemon-pepper seasoning at home! I provide my methodology for making lemon pepper as the second step in the instructions to this recipe.)

Though this braised dish could be made in a crockpot, I much prefer it in my regular conventional oven on a very low heat for several hours! The meat is so tender it will fall off the bone –

but, unlike crockpot or pressure-cooker methods, will stay intact until you can get it to the plate!

For this recipe I usually use my large enamel-coated cast-iron Dutch oven if I'm making this dish to serve four or more people. Anything less than that, it is easily done using a cast-iron skillet for browning and a 9 x 12 casserole dish for the braising. Super-easy is an appropriate description for this recipe. I happen to love green beans, as well as buttered rice with parsley which goes well with this dish. However, as with many stews, this recipe is truly a meal unto itself and needs nothing with it other than a hot, fluffy biscuit with butter! Enjoy!

4 large chicken breasts (intact **with** skin and bone)
3 TABLEspoons olive oil
1 large lemon to provide;
   1 TABLEspoon of lemon zest
   2 TABLEspoons of lemon juice

1 teaspoon each – salt, dry mustard, garlic powder, onion powder
2 teaspoons ground turmeric, ground thyme, fresh finely-minced garlic cloves
3 TABLEspoons ground black pepper
¼ cup corn starch
1 TABLEspoon granulated sugar
3 cups water
1 teaspoon Worcestershire sauce
3 stalks celery (cut into 3-inch julienne strips)
3 whole carrots (peeled and cut into 3-inch stewing pieces)

~ III ~ Fly Away Home

2 large russet baking potatoes (peeled and cut into stewing chunks)
1 large parsnip (peeled, split-cut, then cut into 4 pieces)
2 cups sliced mushrooms
2 medium-size white onions (peeled and quartered with ends intact)

Instructions:

1. Preheat oven at 500°.
2. Using a zester/micro planer – zest the lemon and set zest aside in a small bowl. Add the 3 TABLEspoons of ground black pepper, and 1 teaspoon of salt, stir to combine. Add the turmeric, garlic powder, onion powder, turmeric, thyme. Sprinkle over the chicken breast and let sit for 10 minutes.
3. Using a hand juicer, juice the lemon after you zest the skin—remove any seeds. If the lemon does not yield a full 2 TABLEspoons of juice, you may need to juice half of a second lemon. Pour into a small bowl.
4. Add the cornstarch to the lemon juice and stir. You will have a thick paste. Using a mini-whisk or two salad-forks, stir in the water slowly until you have a milky-looking liquid! Stir in the sugar and Worcestershire sauce. Set this *"slurry"* aside.
5. Heat cast-iron skillet until very hot. Add 3 TABLEspoons of olive oil and immediately turn heat down to medium. Add chicken breasts skin-side down and slowly cook until skin is golden

brown (Do NOT fully cook the chicken — you only want to brown the skin!).

6. Removed browned chicken breast, and then add fresh-minced garlic cloves and mushrooms to Dutch Oven and sauté for 2 minutes. Now, add all the cut up veggies (celery, potatoes, onion, carrots, parsnip).
7. Place the browned chicken breast on top of all the veggies.
8. Pour the slurry over the chicken and veggies.
9. Cover the Dutch Oven, and place in the hot oven. Let cook at 500° for 10 minutes.
10. Turn oven down to 250° and leave in oven to braise for 2 hours.
11. Remove from oven and pour off the braising liquid into the cast-iron skillet and simmer until reduced by at least half. What you want is a thick gravy-type braising liquid for serving.
12. (Shortcut: You can also add ¼ cup additional cornstarch to poured-off braising liquid and cook until thick!)

Roast Pork
(with Apricot/Plum Glaze)

Pre-heat oven and bake on 350°

For the roast:
1 two-pound boneless pork roast loin

The seasoning dust
1 tablespoon all-purpose flour
1 teaspoon each salt, ground black pepper, garlic powder

For the glaze:
6 medium apricots (pitted and quartered)
6 large dark black-purple plums – (pitted and quartered)
½ large white onion
2 cups sugar
5 cups water

½ cup white vinegar
2 tablespoons yellow prepared table mustard (do *NOT*
use a fancy Dijon-type)
1 teaspoon each -- salt, ground black pepper
½ teaspoon ground cinnamon

Instructions:

1. In a small cup, blend together the flour, ground black pepper and garlic powder and liberally dust the meat. Set aside on a meat rack on foiled-lined roasting pan and let seasoning dust adhere to the meat for about 10 minutes or so.
2. In a medium-large sauce pot, add apricots and plums with 2 cups of sugar and 5 cups of water. Bring to a rapid hard boil, then immediately turn down heat to a moderate simmer. Simmer until liquid has reduced by half. (Fruit should be very soft, shiny and liquid almost a soft-ball stage syrup consistency.) Then set aside to cool for about 10 minutes.
3. Using a slotted spoon, remove fruit from liquid and put in a blender. Add the vinegar, mustard, salt, pepper, cinnamon, ½ cup water and puree.
4. Pour puree into stock pot with the reduced liquid and using a whisk, stir to blend. Set aside and let cool. (This glaze should be dark burgundy, very glossy and the consistency of heavy cream!) If it is not glossy, you did not let the sugar cook long enough.
5. Pour ½ cup water in the foil-lined roasting pan. Put meat in oven to roast for 45 minutes. (Turn off the oven at this point.) Remove the meat from the oven, then paint glaze on all sides of meat and return to oven – close the door and allow the remaining heat in the oven to adhere the glaze to the meat.

6. For any remaining juices/water in the foiled-lined roasting pan, pour into a side bowl with the remaining glaze, combine with a whisk and serve as a side-sauce for the meat!

Ali Baba
Persian Rice

The catalyst for creating this recipe were fond memories of my childhood Saturday mornings watching movies of Ali Baba and the Forty Thieves; Aladdin and the Lamp; and all such other wonderful times of magic carpets and such that little boys imagine riding during the pre-teen years of elementary school!

You will need a large fry-pan or wok for the sauté finish!

2 tablespoons olive oil

½ cup each (chopped);
 medium white onion
pistachio nuts (raw or roasted salted will work)
finely diced celery
finely diced red bell pepper
dried apricot
dried-sugared dates
yellow raisins
dark raisins or currants

Spice mixture, 1 teaspoon each –- salt, black pepper, cumin, nutmeg, cinnamon, ground cloves, red pepper flakes, parsley

~ III ~ Fly Away Home

zest of 1 orange (should yield 1 ½ TABLEspoons)
1 orange sectioned (I use a seedless such as Navel)

⅓ cup uncooked long-grain rice
1 TABLEspoon turmeric
3 cups of water

and separately;
⅔ cups uncooked long-grain rice
4 cups of water

and separately,
2 TABLEspoons of water

**I do a short cut with the rice! I cook it in my microwave
then rinse with very cold water as I would pasta!**

Instructions:

1.   In one microwave-safe dish, add ⅔cups of long-grain white rice and 4 cups of water. Cook on high for 12 minutes. Immediately pour rice and liquid through a sifter/strainer and allow cold running water to rinse and cool the cooked rice. Then set aside in a small bowl until needed for last step.
2.   In one microwave-safe dish, add ⅓cup of long-grain white rice, 1 TABLEspoon of turmeric and 3 cups of water. Cook on high for 10 minutes. Immediately pour rice and liquid through a sifter/strainer and allow cold running water to

rinse and cool the cooked rice. Then set aside in a small bowl until needed for last step.

3. Pre-heat your wok or large sauté pan until very, very hot. Then add 2 tablespoons of olive oil. Immediately turn heat down to medium.

4. Add the onion, celery, red bell pepper and slowly sauté until tender. Do not over cook! Do not allow the onions to caramelize! Once tender, add the apricot, dates, raisins, currents and stir-fry for 1 minute (just long enough to heat up)!

5. Sprinkle spice mixture over stir-fried veggies, fruits and nuts.

6. Add the yellow turmeric rice as well as the white long-grain rice simultaneously. Allow to heat up for about 2 minutes.

7. Immediately sprinkly the orange zest atop the rice; add 2 tablespoons of water, and the orange sections. Cover and _remove from heat_. Allow to set aside covered for at least 10 minutes.

The Author

~ o0o ~

J. D. McDuffie learned his cooking skills from two ladies that were sensational southern cooks: His mother and her older sister, a home economist!

From a young child he has always been fascinated with the preparation of food, and began cooking and creating dishes as a teenager. As he traveled about the world during the early years of his career as a CPA and junior corporate finance executive, he recognized the differences yet familiarities of food among the world cuisines.

He begins this book *Ham Bones* as a first volume in a series. He starts with the foundation dishes that he became familiar with as a young child from his ancestors on the farms of South Carolina. He carries the reader through his journey of changes to dishes as well as the development of new dishes as a result of his life's experiences.

The short description of the dishes before the recipe provides humor and an intimate look into his family's living rooms, dining rooms and kitchens as well as their travels to community events such as church union meetings.

J. D. McDuffie writes cookbooks during his retirement years and continues to cook for family and friends for sheer enjoyment!

Index

CPSIA information can be obtained at www.ICGtesting.com
Printed in the USA
BVOW02*0835261215

430920BV00009B/312/P